DINING
THROUGH
THE
SEASONS

JUSTIN BROWN

FOREWORD

I first met Justin in 2006 when we took over the Mermaid Inn near Peterborough. I was Executive Chef at Merchant Inns and Justin had just come back from travelling and wanted a job near his mum's house. He was in his early 20's, had bleached blonde hair and was maybe a bit scruffy but you could see he knew what he wanted to achieve in life and I liked that about him.

He was such a talented chef and it was just a small country pub, so he was a bit wasted there. We quickly took him to the Horse and Groom in Wiltshire which was a bigger pub and more suited to his ability.

We worked together pretty closely back then, designing the menus and dealing with suppliers and I always found Justin a really laid back guy. He was organised and had great attention to detail, which you need if you're going to make it as a chef, but had this calm demeanour which made him really easy to work with.

In those days we had great fun; I remember some supplier trips to Looe in Cornwall, Billingsgate Market and Aubrey Allen in Coventry which really helped me to get to know Justin. He was always full of ideas for dishes and I think we worked well together – I guess I taught him a lot – but he always had this style of producing simple but really good food himself.

He was a big success at The Horse and Groom, so after a year or so, we moved him to The Carnarvon Arms near Newbury which was bigger again; 28 rooms and a 110-seater restaurant. Justin adapted really well, and as ever, just got on with it.

Since he left, we've always kept in touch. I'm pleased he's doing so well now but he's still young and I'm sure has lots more to achieve.

This book captures his cooking perfectly. His food is sophisticated in terms of the flavour but actually quite simple and ideal for the home cook with a passion for food.

The photography is fantastic and Justin has really thought about ways of making it easy for the cook whilst still creating restaurant quality dishes. And importantly, his passion for British produce and supporting local suppliers really shines through in his cooking. Like he says, it's important to let the food do the talking.

Enjoy.

Chef Rob Clayton
Head Chef at Clayton's Kitchen @ The Porter

DINING THROUGH THE SEASONS

©2014 Meze Publishing & Justin Brown.
All rights reserved.

First edition printed in 2014 in the UK.

ISBN: 978-0-9928981-1-3

Written: Justin Brown, Carl Reid

Edited: Phil Turner, James Highmore, Rachel Heward

Photography: Paul Cocker

Design: Paul Cocker

Contributors: Nick Hallam, Joe Food, Jessica Peace, Kieran Wade, Olivia Riches, Samantha Fielding, Sarah Koriba, Victoria Cox

Published by Meze Publishing

Blind Mice Media Ltd

Unit 1 Beehive Works

Milton Street

Sheffield S3 7WL

www.mezepublishing.co.uk

Tel: 0114 275 7709

Justin and his kitchen brigade at the Fifield Inn.

CONTENTS

SPRING

STARTERS

Wye Valley asparagus served with a wild garlic
mayonnaise and toasted cobnuts

Hand-picked crab salad
with a chilled crab bisque and sorrel

Ceviche of the freshest sea bass,
strawberry and citrus

Homemade bread
with homemade whipped butter and sea salt

MAINS

Posh fish pie

Slow cooked pork belly with a chargrilled cauliflower
purée, rosti potato and a pork and onion sauce

Roast breast of free range chicken with morels,
purple sprouting broccoli and a chicken sauce

Lincolnshire Poacher croquette,
garden pea velouté and fresh pea shoots

DESSERTS

Pink champagne granita

Lemon tart with a crème fraîche sorbet

White chocolate mousse with meringue and
poached rhubarb

An English cheeseboard with homemade crackers
and a red onion marmalade

SUMMER

STARTERS

Heirloom tomato salad with sheep's yoghurt,
dried black olive and rocket

Summer garden vegetable salad

Lettuce gazpacho

Cured and confit salmon, cucumber,
dill and a horseradish cream

MAINS

BBQ mackerel, radish, grilled baby gem lettuce
and Japanese mayonnaise

Honey glazed duck breast, pak choi,
roast peach and duck sauce

Fish and chips: Beer battered cod cheek,
crispy fries, tartare sauce and crushed peas

Butter poached pollack, marsh samphire,
mussels and a butter sauce

DESSERTS

Vanilla bean panna cotta with a chilled raspberry
and lemongrass soup

Frozen aerated milk chocolate parfait
with fresh cherries

Strawberries and cream: Vanilla cream,
strawberry jelly and fresh strawberries

Berries and snow:
Fresh summer berries with frozen yoghurt

AUTUMN

STARTERS

Canapés: Seed meringues and oat biscuits
with sour cream, herbs and flowers

Crispy pigs' ears with a bramley apple sauce

A broth of autumn mushrooms and soy

Deep fried rock oyster in panko breadcrumbs,
duck ham and apple

MAINS

Rainbow trout with a watercress purée, shaved
fennel, grilled baby leek and trout roe

Double cooked shoulder of lamb with
heritage carrots, runner beans and a lamb sauce

Wild mushroom risotto,
pickled mushroom and fresh black truffle

Five spice duck breast with a celeriac purée and kale

DESSERTS

Sticky toffee pudding with a sticky toffee sauce

Passion fruit crème brûlée with a shortbread biscuit

Old fashioned plum cobbler

Caramelised rice pudding

WINTER

STARTERS

Cauliflower soup with an onion bhaji

Pan fried breast of wood pigeon,
shallot and thyme tatin and a pigeon sauce

Poached duck egg with cauliflower,
crispy shallot, Parma ham and pea shoots

Hand dived scallop, Jerusalem artichoke purée
and winter truffle

MAINS

Poached guinea fowl breast, parsnip purée,
grilled baby leek and a Madeira sauce

Slow cooked pork belly, turnip purée,
roast plum and turnip tops

Beef fillet, burnt onion and roast parsnip
with a red wine and thyme sauce

Oven-roasted Cornish cod, cauliflower and pearl
barley couscous, roasted cobnuts, home dried raisins
and a Sauternes sauce

DESSERTS

Dark chocolate and hazelnut fondant,
muesli, chocolate soil and frozen yoghurt

Peanut butter mousse,
toasted hazelnuts and glazed banana

Brown sugar cake with a butterscotch sauce

Poached baby pear,
coconut pudding and hazelnut praline

MEET JUSTIN BROWN

I was 16 when I first started thinking about a career in food. I'd finished school and, to be honest, university was never an option for me. I also knew I didn't have the attention span for an office job. I had big ambitions – but didn't really know where to go with them. All I knew was it had to be something creative. That's why I started writing off to every five star deluxe hotel in London saying how I was interested in working in a kitchen. If a job's worth doing, it's worth doing well, right?

Luckily, The Landmark London Hotel in Marylebone got back to me and offered me an apprenticeship – it was the start of an incredible culinary journey. I also enrolled for one day a week at City of Westminster College. During my time at The Landmark I became fully qualified and honed my craft.

I was offered a job at a private members' club in South Kensington owned by Ronnie Wood of The Rolling Stones called the Harrington Club. The head chef there was Arthur Potts Dawson (who was also the nephew of Mick Jagger). It was an amazing experience. Arthur had previously worked with Jamie Oliver at The River Café and, when he heard that Jamie was looking for chefs in Knightsbridge, he recommended me. That's when things went crazy. I was working with renowned Australian chef Ben O'Donoghue and it was just a different world. Everyone went there, I mean everyone! We'd have the Beckhams in, Madonna, Guy Richie, all the footballers. It was amazing – and it was then that I knew I wanted to be more than an anonymous chef behind the scenes.

After a couple of years, my itchy feet saw me heading off on some extended jollies. I'd had five years in London, achieved a hell of a lot in a short space of time, and simply wanted to see what else was out there. Thailand, Hawaii, New Zealand, America – I did the lot, ate a lot and learned a lot, for about 18 months.

Coming home, I didn't have a plan. I was skint, unemployed – but I knew my previous experience would see me land on my feet. I took a chef job in my local pub, little did I know it would turn out to be one of the best moves of my career so far as it was owned by Robert Breare – who was in the process of setting up Merchant Inns.

A stint at The Mermaid in Ellington, Cambridgeshire followed before I was offered the head chef position at The Horse and Groom in Charlton, Wiltshire – and it was here that I started to get recognised.

We made the Michelin Guide and picked up a whole bunch of awards in the first year. It was a trend which would follow me around. A move to The Carnarvon Arms in Newbury saw us hitting the Michelin Guide every year I was there – and I personally picked up a Pub Chef of the Year award three years on the trot.

A certain Andrew Lloyd Webber ate regularly at The Carnarvon Arms. Some friends of his were investors who were looking to open some restaurants with a chef and Andrew recommended me. Our first venture, The Sun Inn, Dummer, saw us picking up 1AA Rosette and making the Michelin Guide within our first three months – as well as picking up Best Newcomer Pub at the Great British Pub Awards. Farringford on the Isle of Wight swiftly followed – a beautiful old manor house once owned by famed poet Lord Tennyson. This time we gained 2AA Rosettes and mentions in the Good Food and Michelin Guides, all within three months.

With everything going so well, it was inevitable that my itchy feet would kick in again – so it was a busman's holiday to Australia. What can I say … it made sense to me.

They don't have stars over there, they have hats – and I landed myself a job working in Restaurant Amusé, Perth – an amazing three hat restaurant that didn't even offer diners a menu. You'd get what you were given – and it was packed every night. Further travelling followed – and, to be honest, I could write a book about those experiences alone. I was also fortunate enough to spend time with Attica, Melbourne.

I've got all that out of my system now. Honest. But, needless to say, all of this has shaped me into the chef I am today.

It's time for my next chapter … and for you to turn to the first.

THIS
BOOK

I'd had the idea for this book for some time. My friends and family are always hosting gatherings and often ask me for ideas and recipes – so this is as much for them as anyone else (it'll give me a bit of peace).

Everyone likes to cook seasonally, but I wanted to create something you could turn to for simple yet amazing recipes whatever the season.

The great thing about this book is most dishes can be prepared in advance – meaning, by the time your guests arrive, all your hard work is done! It'll give you more time to spend actually enjoying the occasion – and less time panicking about it!

It's sticking to what I do best; big-tasting dishes that aren't overcomplicated yet offer that 'wow' factor. I want to show you just how easy some complicated looking dishes can be and let you in on a few tricks of the trade while I'm at it.

So, forget the stress and the thought process. It's all in here.

Enjoy being the host with the most … whatever the season!

SPRING

Spring for me is the start of a new year. The weather is beginning to turn, Christmas is long forgotten and a new season is upon us bringing new inspiration, produce and ideas.

The beginning of Spring brings out all the beautiful green produce which is great in flavour, good for us and brings life and colour to the plate.

Succulent asparagus, peppery watercress, pungent wild garlic, gorgeous purple sprouting broccoli and don't forget the lovely spring lamb, wood pigeon, beautiful fresh crab and trout – all readily available to us.

It really is a season to get excited about and it always puts a big smile on my face, so why not go down to your local market, see all this amazing produce the season has to offer and start cooking this delicious food whilst the season is upon us.

WYE VALLEY ASPARAGUS SERVED WITH A WILD GARLIC MAYONNAISE AND TOASTED COBNUTS

Asparagus and wild garlic are perfect at this time of the year, a real celebration of what the UK has to offer. Add the toasted cobnuts for texture and I'm sure you'll agree, this is a great way to start a meal with a dish full of flavour, colour and life.

Ingredients | Serves 4-6

18 asparagus spears

60g cobnuts

For the mayonnaise

60g wild garlic leaves

3 free range egg yolks

300ml virgin olive oil (approximately)

1 teaspoon white wine vinegar

Sea salt and pepper

½ lemon, juiced

I use three or four asparagus spears per portion so you can adjust the amount of asparagus needed depending on how many people you are cooking for. Take the asparagus and cut off roughly half an inch off the bottom to remove the tough woody part, then take a peeler and peel the bottom inch of each spear. Bring a pan of water up to the boil with a pinch of sea salt, take the asparagus and cook them in the boiling water for 2 minutes. Remove the asparagus and plunge straight into iced water; this will stop the cooking process and keep the asparagus bright in colour. Once cool, remove the asparagus and keep them on a cloth until needed.

For the mayonnaise, remove the stalks from the wild garlic, plunge them into a pan of salted boiling water for 5 seconds then remove the leaves with a slotted spoon and plunge straight into iced water to stop the cooking process. Once cooled remove and squeeze out the excess water. In a tall jug, place the egg yolks, white wine vinegar and lemon juice; take a stick blender and blitz for a minute. Then very slowly add the olive oil, blitzing constantly and the egg will slowly emulsify with the oil forming a mayonnaise. This will thicken very quickly and may not require all the oil. Once the mayonnaise thickens add the wild garlic leaves, season and blitz again for a minute until bright in colour. The mayonnaise will turn a lovely green and is now ready to serve.

For the cobnuts, crush them with a rolling pin between a cloth but don't break them too much. Transfer them to a baking tray and toast them gently for a few minutes under a grill and leave to cool.

Chef's Tip

If you do not own a stick blender you can also make this in a tall liquidiser. If for some reason your mayonnaise was to split, this is usually caused by adding the oil too fast. Just add one tablespoon of warm water and blitz again and this will bind your mayonnaise back together.

To Serve

Take your spears of asparagus and season with salt, pepper and drizzle with a little olive oil. Either serve cold, or place in a frying pan with a knob of butter and gently warm through. Place onto your plates, spoon some mayonnaise next to the spears and sprinkle over the toasted cobnuts.

HAND-PICKED CRAB SALAD WITH A CHILLED CRAB BISQUE AND SORREL

The common brown crab is one of the most popular varieties in the UK and at this time of year they are in season and perfect to eat; the flesh is so tasty and easy to pick from the shell. This dish is all about the crab, celebrating every part of it and really highlighting its natural flavour.

Ingredients | Serves 4-6

For the crab

1 live brown crab, 1kg in weight

For the chilled crab bisque

500g crab shells

500g langoustine shells

2 star anise

1 cinnamon stick

5g coriander seeds

5g fennel seeds

2 shallots

1 head of garlic, split

2 sticks lemon grass, broken with the back of a knife

50g tomato purée

2 litres water

100ml double cream

For the garnish

Sorrel leaves

1 lemon

Olive oil

Sea salt and pepper

Speak to your local fishmonger – they will always be able to get live crabs – but if you don't feel comfortable preparing one yourself, they'll be able to get you some handpicked crabmeat instead. About 500g of white crab meat and 100g of brown crab meat would be enough to serve 4-6 people. Just make sure you get the crab shells and langoustine shells as well, about 500g of each will be enough to make a nice rich sauce.

Take the crab and freeze it for 30 minutes, this will help calm it down. Bring a large pan of water to the boil and add a pinch of salt. Take the crab and kill it by placing a skewer through one of the two points in the underside then place it straight into the water. Make sure the crab is completely submerged and boil for 15 minutes. Once cooked, remove the crab from the water and leave it to cool then remove the claws and legs, turn the crab over and remove the body from the shell by pushing it with your thumbs. Remove the dead man's fingers; they will surround the inside of the body when you remove it and any other hard membrane. Discard all of this but keep all of the shell. With a spoon scoop out the brown meat from the main top shell of the crab and keep separate. Then in a bowl use the handle of a spoon to get all of the white meat out of the body. Once you can't get any more meat out, cut the body in half to expose more channels and scoop out the remaining meat. With the back of a heavy knife crack the claws and legs and remove the flesh. Once you have all the meat, pick through it with your

hands to make sure no little bits of shell are left in the crab meat. Once picked-through, refrigerate the brown and white crab meat separately until needed.

For the bisque, take a heavy based saucepan and add a splash of olive oil over a medium heat. Add the shallot, garlic and lemongrass and sweat for 5 minutes, then add the star anise, coriander seeds, cinnamon and fennel seeds and cook for a further 5 minutes. Once the aromas start releasing add the tomato purée and shellfish bones, sweat for 5 more minutes and using a wooden spoon crush them up as much as you can. Once you've done this add the water and boil for an hour to intensify the sauce. When reduced by half add the double cream and simmer for a further half an hour until the sauce thickens, enough to lightly cover the back of a spoon. Turn off the heat and leave to cool for 30 minutes. Once cooled, strain the sauce through a fine sieve using a wooden spoon to push through as much sauce as you can, then keep the sauce and discard all the shells from the pan. Chill until needed.

To Serve

Place the brown crab meat into one bowl and the white into another. Season both meats with half a lemon (juiced), sea salt, pepper and a drizzle of olive oil. Give the meat a thorough mix with all the ingredients. In each bowl place a spoon of brown crab meat, top with the white crab meat and pour the crab bisque around the meat. Garnish with a few sorrel leaves and serve straight away.

CEVICHE OF THE FRESHEST SEA BASS, STRAWBERRY AND CITRUS

This dish requires the freshest sea bass you can find. Ceviche is a marinade of fresh citrus juices which is used to cure the fresh fish, the acid in the citrus will start to cook the fish and change the texture leaving you with the most amazing freshness on the plate.

Ingredients | Serves 4-6

650g freshest sea bass

50g strawberries

Baby salad leaves to garnish

For the citrus cure

1 lemon

1 grapefruit

1 orange

1 lime

Salt and pepper

2 tablespoons olive oil

This is a really simple and fresh starter which requires the freshest of ingredients. Let's start with the fish. Go down to your local fishmonger and speak to them, they will make sure they give you the best quality sea bass they have. Get them to fillet, remove the pin bones and skin the fish for you. Place the cold fillet on a chopping board and with a sharp knife slice the fish diagonally through the fillet no more than 1 cm thick until you have sliced the whole fillet. Once you have your pieces, divide them onto 4-6 plates and arrange nicely.

For the cure, squeeze the juice of the lemon, grapefruit, orange and lime through a fine sieve to remove any pips and fibres that may fall out. Then take the juice, add the olive oil, season with salt and pepper and mix. Taste and make sure you're happy with the seasoning then chill until required.

To Serve

Once you've arranged the fish on the plate, drizzle over the citrus cure and leave to marinade for 5 minutes. Whilst the fish is marinating, take the strawberries and slice thinly with a knife, place over the fish, garnish with a few salad leaves and serve.

HOMEMADE BREAD WITH HOMEMADE WHIPPED BUTTER AND SEA SALT

I love the smell of fresh bread coming out of the oven… you just can't beat it. Match that with homemade butter and it goes to show it's the simple things in life done properly that always come out on top.

Ingredients | Serves 4-6

For the bread

750g white bread flour

400ml tepid water

35g fresh yeast

40g unsalted butter

20g fine salt

100ml olive oil

2 whole eggs

For the butter

2 litres double cream

Specialist equipment

Thermo whip, 2 cream chargers

Before we start I would just like to explain about the thermo whip. They are widely available and relatively cheap, so if you can I would suggest investing in one, but if you do not own one of these the butter is equally delicious without it, it will just be a little denser. I use it to whip the butter with the nitrous oxide chargers; when you squeeze out the butter from the thermo whip it will be really light and airy. It's simply delicious.

I think people don't realise how easy it is to make homemade butter. Use an electric mixer, pour the double cream into the bowl, add the whisk attachment and whisk on full. The cream will begin to whip; we are deliberately over-whipping the cream so keep it going, after 5 minutes or so butter milk will start to separate from the cream, just keep whisking the cream on full until the butter sticks to the whisk in a lump and can't be whisked anymore. This will take about 10 minutes.

Remove the whisk and pull off all the butter, I like to keep the buttermilk and use it when I make mashed potato, it's delicious. Place the butter in a bowl of iced water and soak it for 5 minutes. Take it out and with your hands try and squeeze out anymore buttermilk. The more we get rid of the longer the butter will last, usually about 7 days. When you have squeezed out the butter place it in a container and put in the fridge. Your butter is ready. Simple as that.

For the bread, put all the ingredients into an electric mixer with a dough hook and mix on a high speed for 7 minutes. Once the dough has formed tip it into a floured bowl, cover with a damp cloth and leave it in a warm place to rise for 30 minutes. Once risen, flour a work surface and tip out the dough. With the dough you have a few options; either cut it into six pieces and roll into balls to make bread rolls, keep it as a whole and make an oblong shape to make a bloomer or place it in a 500g floured loaf tin to make a loaf, it's up to you. I like to make a whole bloomer so once you have your dough get a baking tray and line with greaseproof paper, flour and put the dough on the tray. Cover with a damp cloth again and leave in a warm place for about 30 minutes until the dough has doubled in size. Once the bread has doubled in size you have a few more options; you can leave the bread plain, flour the top of the loaf or sprinkle poppy seeds or sesame seeds over the top, it's entirely up to you. If you are making a loaf, preheat your oven to 220°c and cook for about 25 minutes until the bread is golden brown. Lift up the bread with a cloth after 25 minutes, tap the bottom of the loaf and if it sounds hollow it is ready. If you are making six bread rolls cook them for just 15 minutes. Once the bread is cooked take out of the oven and leave to cool on a cake rack.

To Serve

Take out the butter from the fridge a few hours before your guests arrive so the butter gets up to room temperature. Once at room temperature spoon about 350g into a thermo whip, charge it with one canister and shake, remove the canister and charge it with another and shake again for a few minutes. Point the nozzle into a serving bowl, gently squeeze and the butter will come out like a butter foam. Sprinkle with sea salt. Warm your loaf of bread for 5 minutes in an oven preheated to 180°c. Once warm, slice and serve with the butter.

If you did not used a thermo whip, leave the butter out until it gets to room temperature then spoon into a serving dish, sprinkle with sea salt and serve.

POSH FISH PIE

I'm calling this dish posh fish pie. Why? Gone are the days when you need to cook all the fish together in a pie dish; the fish overcooks and the colours fade, so I've given it a 21st century makeover. Cooking each element of the pie separately and perfectly assembling at the last minute.

Ingredients | Serves 6

For the filling

300ml fish sauce

400g pollack fillet

400g salmon fillet

1 fillet natural undyed smoked haddock

100ml whole milk

olive oil

For the topping

150g panko breadcrumbs

150g grated Lincolnshire Poacher cheese

8 Maris Piper potatoes

50g unsalted butter

70ml double cream

Salt and pepper

For the garnish

½ bunch dill

This dish requires no real planning in advance except for sourcing the ingredients. Go to your local fishmonger and get them to fillet, skin and pin bone the pollack and salmon. For the smoked haddock, get a natural undyed fillet which I think are far better than the yellow dyed fillets. Keep the skin on the fillet but get the pin bones removed (you can do this yourself by running your fingers along the flesh and when you feel the bones, removing them with fish tweezers). Cut the salmon into about twelve pieces, do exactly the same with the pollack and this will give you about two pieces of each fish per portion.

Tip the milk into a pan and add the smoked haddock fillet, bring the milk up to a simmer and simmer for 6 minutes. Turn off the heat and leave the fish in the milk.

For the topping, peel and dice the potatoes, place in a pan and cover with water. Add a pinch of salt and boil until tender. Once cooked strain in a colander. In another pan heat the cream and butter, add the potatoes and mash. Once mashed, really beat them with a wooden spoon to mix everything together, season with salt and pepper and keep warm. I like to place my mashed potato in a piping bag, it will keep warm for a good 15 minutes and it's great for presentation when piping the mash on to the plate.

Take the panko breadcrumbs and toast them gently under a grill until golden brown. Tip them into a bowl and allow to cool, then add the grated cheese and mix. I use panko breadcrumbs because they are very crispy and give a good texture to the dish and if you don't have Lincolnshire Poacher you can always substitute with grated Parmesan cheese.

For the sauce follow the steps for the fish sauce recipe in the basics section, take your fish sauce out the fridge and bring to a gentle simmer in a pan.

To cook the pollack and salmon take a large frying pan and heat some olive oil over a high heat. Season the fish with sea salt and pepper then add the pieces of pollack and salmon to the pan and cook for 3 minutes until golden. Turn the pieces over and cook for a further minute. Once cooked, turn off the heat.

To Serve

Place two pieces of salmon and two pieces of pollack into each bowl, take the smoked haddock out of the milk and flake the meat evenly into each bowl. Spoon the fish sauce over the fish. If the fish sauce is too thick then thin it down slightly with some of the smoked haddock poaching milk. Next, pipe on the mashed potato then sprinkle over the crunchy cheese and breadcrumb mix and add a few sprigs of dill. I think once you try this version you'll never go back.

SLOW COOKED PORK BELLY WITH A CHARGRILLED CAULIFLOWER PURÉE, ROSTI POTATO AND A PORK AND ONION SAUCE

With this dish, the pork belly needs 24 hours to set so forward planning is essential. Cook the meat the day before your dinner party then all you have to worry about when your guests arrive is the finishing touches.

Ingredients | Serves 6

1½kg pork belly, skin removed

4 star anise

5g sea salt

5g peppercorns

5g coriander seeds

1 bay leaf

For the rosti potato

5 Maris Piper potatoes

½ bunch thyme

Sea salt and pepper

Knob of butter

For the cauliflower purée

1 cauliflower

200ml whole milk

100ml double cream

5g butter

For the pork and onion sauce

100ml white wine

Pork belly juices

1 large white onion

100ml double cream

½ lemon

Ask your butcher to remove the skin from the pork belly and keep it for crackling. In a pestle and mortar grind the sea salt, peppercorns, bay leaf, star anise and coriander seeds then season the top of the pork belly with the rub. Once you have seasoned the meat, take some tin foil and wrap the belly. Preheat the oven to 150°c and place the tin foiled belly into a roasting tray then into the oven for 4 hours. Once roasted, turn the oven off and leave to cool. Once cool, remove the tray and tip any juices into a separate container and save for later. Discard the tin foil then wrap the belly in cling film and place onto a baking tray, putting another baking tray on top. Then put into the fridge. Place something heavy on top of the pork belly like a large milk carton and set in the fridge for a minimum of 12 hours, ideally 24 hours. The idea is to flatten out the belly so when roasted the next day, it will cook evenly. It also helps with the presentation.

For the skin, preheat the oven to 180°c. Take a pair of scissors and cut into ½cm strips. Line the baking tray with greaseproof paper and place the strips on top. Season with sea salt. Cook in the oven for 20 minutes, then put the crackling on a cake rack and leave to dry overnight.

For the rosti potatoes, peel and wash the potatoes then grate into a bowl. Season with salt and pepper, place the grated potato onto a kitchen cloth and squeeze out as much liquid as you can; the more you can squeeze out the crispier your rosti will be so use some force. Pick the thyme leaves off the stalks and add them to the potato mix. Place a small saucepan over a low heat, add a knob of butter and drizzle of olive oil and press in the potato mix so it's about ½cm thick. Cook for 3-4 minutes then flip over and cook for a further 3-4 minutes until you have a golden, crispy rosti potato. Place each rosti on a tray and repeat until you have your required amount.

The charred flavour from the chargrilled cauliflower purée compliments the pork belly really well. Take a whole cauliflower and remove the florets, keeping some of the stalk on the florets. Take a chargrill pan (no oil needed) and place on a medium heat, charring the outside of the florets in the pan. Once charred, transfer them to a heavy based saucepan and add the milk, cream, seasoning and simmer until the cauliflower is soft. Then place in a blender and blend to a smooth purée.

For the sauce, peel and dice the onion and cook with a drizzle of olive oil and a knob of butter in a saucepan over a medium heat. Cook for 5 minutes until translucent, add the white wine and reduce by half. Then add the pork belly juices and double cream and reduce by half again. Once that's done, blitz with a hand blender to incorporate the onion and season with black pepper and a squeeze of lemon juice.

Chef's Tip

If you don't own a chargrill make the purée without chargrilling. Once the purée is made, heat 30g of butter in a saucepan over a medium heat until it starts to brown, known as a beurre noisette. Once brown, add the cauliflower purée to the pan and mix in the nut brown butter, this will give you an equally delicious purée.

To Serve

Remove the pork belly from the fridge, unwrap and slice into 4-6 portions. In a frying pan, heat a tablespoon of olive oil over a medium heat, place the belly pieces in skin side down and brown for a few minutes. Once complete, transfer to a tray and heat through a preheated oven at 180°c for 10 minutes to warm through. You can also heat your rosti potatoes on a tray for a few minutes if made in advance. Place the rosti central on a plate, spoon the purée on the rosti, place the pork belly on top, then drizzle over the sauce and serve with a piece of crackling. A pork lover's dream.

ROAST BREAST OF FREE RANGE CHICKEN WITH MORELS, PURPLE SPROUTING BROCCOLI AND A CHICKEN SAUCE

Go down to your local vegetable market or greengrocers and pick up some morel mushrooms, they are delicious and must be tried during this time of year; a perfect combination with the roast chicken breast.

Ingredients | Serves 4-6

4-6 free range chicken breasts

250g morel mushrooms

16 purple sprouting broccoli stems

500ml chicken sauce (page 124)

20g butter

Olive oil

10ml white wine

Salt and pepper

The quality of your chicken breasts is essential here; so speak to your local butcher and look for a decent quality local free range chicken breast with the skin and wing bone still attached. Ask the butcher to French trim the breast and they will clean the bone for you.

Preheat the oven to 180°c. Place a large non-stick frying pan over a medium heat, season each chicken breast with sea salt and pepper and rub with olive oil. Place the breasts skin side down in the pan and cook for 5 minutes to crisp the skin, making sure you do not burn the chicken, so every now and then use some tongs to check and adjust the heat if needed. After 5 minutes flip over the chicken and seal the bottom for 1 minute. Transfer the chicken breasts to a baking tray and place in the oven and roast for 12 minutes. Remove from the oven, cover in foil and rest for 10 minutes.

The broccoli can be cooked moments before serving. Put a saucepan on the stove, fill with water and bring to the boil, adding a pinch of salt. Once boiling, add the purple sprouting broccoli and cook for 3 minutes. This type of broccoli is so tender and delicious that you do not need to trim the stalks which are so thin; they won't require more than 3 minutes to cook. Once cooked, strain and place them on a cloth to remove any excess water.

The morels may have some dirt on them and the best way to clean them is with a pastry brush. Just brush the outside of each one and give them a little tap in case any dirt has made its way inside them. In a saucepan, heat the butter and a little olive oil over a medium to high heat. Add the mushroom and sauté for 2 minutes, stirring every few seconds, then add the white wine and cook for a further 2 minutes until it has evaporated. Season with salt and pepper. Once the mushrooms begin to soak up the butter and the wine has evaporated they will soften. Once softened, tip them onto some kitchen paper to remove any excess liquid.

Heat the chicken sauce over a medium heat until it simmers.

To Serve

This is a really simple dish but using the best produce available and that's what we are celebrating in this meal. Place the chicken breast on your plate, arrange some purple sprouting broccoli and scatter around the morels, drizzle over some sauce and you're ready to serve.

LINCOLNSHIRE POACHER CROQUETTE, GARDEN PEA VELOUTÉ AND FRESH PEA SHOOTS

This is one of my favourite vegetarian meals, such a simple dish but I think the smoothness of the velouté matched with the crispy croquette and the fresh pea shoots complement each other perfectly.

Ingredients | Serves 6

For the croquettes
280g Lincolnshire Poacher cheese
100g panko breadcrumbs
200g mashed potato (approximately 4 Maris Piper potatoes)
3 egg yolks
1 bunch of chives

For the croquette coating
5 whole eggs
100g panko breadcrumbs
100g plain flour
Vegetable oil for frying

For the pea velouté
1kg frozen peas
Water to cover
Sea salt and pepper
½ lemon
½ white onion
1 bulb of garlic
5g butter

For the garnish
1 punnet of peashoots

Start with the pea velouté by finely dicing the onion and garlic and placing into a heavy based saucepan. Add the butter and a few tablespoons of olive oil, place the pan over a medium heat and sweat for 5 minutes but make sure there is no colour on the onions and garlic. Once nice and translucent add the peas and coat in the onion mix, add hot water straight from a kettle and cover the peas. As soon as it starts to boil remove the pan from the heat and liquidise with either a stick blender or a liquidiser. Once blended, season with lemon juice, salt and pepper and chill in a container until needed.

To make the croquettes, start by grating the cheese into a mixing bowl, if you don't have Lincolnshire Poacher then a strong cheddar cheese will do the trick. To the grated cheese add the cold mash potato, (about four Maris Piper potatoes boiled, mashed and cooled will be enough), finely chopped chives, breadcrumbs, egg yolks and generously season with sea salt and black pepper. Put on some rubber gloves and mix the mixture as well as you can for a few minutes until everything is incorporated together. Once mixed check the seasoning then shape the mix into croquettes, about three per portion – 4cm long and 1cm diameter will do the job nicely. Once moulded, put them on a tray and chill in the fridge for an hour to firm slightly.

Whilst the croquettes are in the fridge take three bowls so we can breadcrumb them once they have chilled. In one bowl add some plain flour, in the second crack the eggs and whisk together and in the last bowl add the breadcrumbs. Take the croquettes out of the fridge, place each one in the flour and coat them, patting any excess flour off. Coat them in the egg mix, place in the breadcrumbs and coat evenly; the breadcrumbs will stick and cover the croquette completely. Chill in the fridge on a tray until needed.

To Serve

If you have a deep fat fryer fill it with vegetable oil, set it to 180°c and fry the croquettes for 5 minutes. If you don't have a fryer, place a deep frying pan on the stove and fill it with about 1cm of vegetable oil to shallow fry the croquettes. Once the oil is warm add the croquettes and fry for 5 minutes turning every minute until golden brown. Remove from the oil and drain on some paper towels. Take the pea velouté from the fridge and warm gently in a pan for a few minutes. Tip the velouté into the bottom of a bowl, add the crispy croquettes and garnish with pea shoots. To add another element to the dish try with a poached hen's or duck egg, the croquettes act like soldiers for the runny egg yolk. Give it a try and see what you think.

PINK CHAMPAGNE GRANITA

Granitas are a great way to finish a meal. The refreshing ice crystals will cleanse your palate leaving you feeling cool on a hot summer's day.

Ingredients | Serves 6

For the granita

220g sugar

750ml pink champagne

500ml water

1 lemon

For the garnish

Mint leaves

This is a really easy dessert to make; it can be made in advance and will keep in the freezer for 2 months. It's great served on fresh fruit although in the restaurant I serve it in a shot glass as a palate cleanser between courses.

To make the granita, place the water and sugar into a heavy based saucepan and bring to the boil. Simmer for 5 minutes then take it off the heat and leave to cool. When cool, pop open the bottle of pink champagne and add to the cool sugar syrup, add the juice of the lemon, whisk everything together and tip into a plastic container.

Place a lid on and put into the freezer. For the first 4 hours take out the granita every hour and with a fork mash the ice crystals together to stop then forming into one big block, it's good to break them into as little pieces as possible. After the fourth time of scraping and mixing leave in the freezer until needed.

To Serve

Take the granita out of the freezer and using a fork scrape the crystals and break them up. Spoon into a bowl, garnish with a few mint leaves and serve straight away before it melts.

LEMON TART WITH A CRÈME FRAÎCHE SORBET

This is a fantastic end to a meal; the crème fraîche sorbet works really well with the zingy lemon and these days, ice cream machines are very affordable and easy to get hold of. But don't worry if you don't have one, serving it with a simple dollop of crème fraîche will do the job nicely too.

Ingredients | Serves 6	For the pastry	For the crème fraîche sorbet
For the lemon tart filling	220g soft butter	150ml water
6 lemons	125g caster sugar	55g granulated sugar
340g caster sugar	390g plain flour	250g crème fraîche
10 whole eggs	2 egg yolks	Icing sugar, for dusting
1 pint double cream	Flour for dusting	**Specialist equipment**
		Blow torch, ice cream machine

The beauty of this lemon tart mix is that you cook it separately meaning you will guarantee a crispy tart case when you serve. To start the pastry, place the sugar and butter in a large mixing bowl with a paddle attachment and beat until light and creamy, this will take about 5 minutes. Then add the egg yolks and sifted flour and beat on a low speed until a dough forms. Remove the paddle and knead into a ball, wrap it in cling film and rest in the fridge for 2 hours. After 2 hours preheat the oven to 170°c, take a 25cm tart ring or six individual 6cm tart cases and place onto a baking tray lined with greaseproof paper. Roll out the pastry on a floured surface turning the pastry after every roll until it is about ½cm thick then place it over your tart case or cases. Let some excess pastry hang over the edges as it may shrink a little in cooking. Prick the bottom of the pastry with a fork, scrunch some greaseproof paper and line the pastry. Fill it with raw rice to the top and blind bake in the oven for 30 minutes. Remove from the oven, remove the rice and paper and cook for a further 10 minutes to colour and crisp up the base. Leave to cool, trim any excess pastry from around the sides and transfer to a cake rack.

Zest and juice the lemons into a saucepan, add the sugar to the lemon juice and zest and bring to the boil over a high heat. Once boiling, remove from the heat and leave to cool. Crack the eggs into a separate bowl and add the cream to the eggs, whisking together until fully incorporated. Once the lemon mix is cool, strain it through a fine sieve into the egg and cream and whisk together. Tip the lemon tart mix into a deep tray lined with greaseproof paper and cook for 25 minutes at 105°c. After 25 minutes remove the lemon tart mix and allow to cool, then transfer into a plastic container and store in the fridge until needed.

The crème fraîche sorbet is very simple to make but if you do not own an ice cream machine, using crème fraîche on its own is fine. In a saucepan add the sugar and water, bring to the boil. Once boiling leave for 1 minute to dissolve the sugar then turn the heat off and allow to cool. This is called a stock syrup. Once cool, whisk the crème fraîche into the stock syrup and transfer into an ice cream machine. Churn for 20 minutes until the sorbet thickens, then transfer to a plastic container and freeze.

To Serve

Remove the lemon tart mix from the fridge and spoon the thick mixture into your tart case or cases, fill to the top and run a pallet knife along the top of the tart so it's level. Remember we have already cooked the filling so you can fill the tarts just before serving. Once the tart is full and smoothed over, dust with icing sugar and gently caramelise with a blow torch. Place onto a plate and serve with the sorbet or a dollop of crème fraîche.

WHITE CHOCOLATE MOUSSE WITH MERINGUE AND POACHED RHUBARB

This is my ultimate white chocolate mousse recipe, along with the crispy meringue and soft poached rhubarb, it's a dessert lover's dream with great contrasts, colours and textures.

Ingredients | Serves 6

For the meringue

4 organic egg whites

180g caster sugar

For the white chocolate mousse

240g white chocolate

90ml whole milk

1 leaf gelatine

240ml double cream

For the poached rhubarb

6 sticks rhubarb

180g caster sugar

450ml water

50ml cranberry juice

The meringue takes time to cook so this should be made in advance and kept on a cake rack so it stays crisp until needed. In a clean, very dry mixing bowl add the egg whites, put on the whisk attachment and whisk on a high setting until the whites begin to form soft peaks. Once at soft peak stage, add the caster sugar one tablespoon at a time, still whisking fast until you have used all the sugar. You will be left with a stiff meringue. Preheat the oven to 50°c, line a baking tray with greaseproof paper and spread the meringue out over the tray to about ½cm thick. Place in the oven and leave overnight for 8-10 hours. Once crisp, take the meringue out of the oven and leave to completely cool, don't touch it for a good 4 hours. It will be crisp, so place it onto a cake rack and leave until needed.

For the poached rhubarb, place the water, cranberry juice and sugar in a saucepan (the cranberry juice enhances the colour of the rhubarb), bring to the boil to dissolve the sugar then switch off the heat and leave for 10 minutes to cool, this is called a stock syrup. Trim the tops and bottoms of the rhubarb and cut each stick into three. Place in a tray and tip over the stock syrup we just made, leave on the side until the liquid cools completely, the heat in the stock syrup will be enough to gently soften the rhubarb. Once cool place in a container and refrigerate until needed.

Cover the gelatine leaf with cold water and soak for at least 5 minutes. In a pan warm the milk but keep an eye on it; just before it's about to boil take it off the heat. Lift out the now soft gelatine leaf and add to the milk, whisking to dissolve. Place the white chocolate pieces into a bowl and pour over the warm milk. With a wooden spoon mix everything together until the chocolate has melted and everything has incorporated together, leaving to cool. In another bowl, whip the double cream with a whisk until it has reached soft peaks. Take the whipped cream and fold it into the white chocolate with a wooden spoon; be careful not to knock the air out of the dessert. Once incorporated together tip the mousse into a tub and place in the fridge for a minimum of 2 hours.

To Serve

This dessert can be made a day in advance so when you have friends around for dinner you can concentrate on entertaining.

Spoon or pipe the white chocolate mousse onto each plate then add two or three pieces of poached rhubarb per person. Take the meringue and snap into pieces and place on the mousse; this is a really vibrant dessert with some great textures, so enjoy.

AN ENGLISH CHEESEBOARD WITH HOMEMADE CRACKERS AND A RED ONION MARMALADE

Ingredients | Serves 4-6

For the crackers

500g plain flour, sifted

200g whole milk

2 whole eggs

10g salt

10g sugar

40g poppy seeds

40g sesame seeds

For the red onion marmalade

15 red onions

100g soft brown sugar

100ml red wine vinegar

½ bottle red wine

100ml water

1 bay leaf

Olive oil

A knob of butter

Sea salt and cracked black pepper

Cheese selection

200g Cornish Yarg

200g Lincolnshire Poacher

200g Bath Soft

Who doesn't like a cheeseboard to finish a meal? I normally use three British cheeses and about 200g of each cheese will serve four to six people. I have given an example of my favourite cheeses but go down to your local market, have a try and pick some that you like. The addition of homemade crackers and onion marmalade will really impress your friends.

Start by peeling and thinly slicing the red onions. In a heavy based saucepan heat a knob of butter and a drizzle of olive oil and add the red onions, season with sea salt and black pepper then cook them on a high heat for 5 minutes stirring constantly. Season with sea salt and black pepper then add the red wine, water, brown sugar, red wine vinegar and bay leaf to the onions, stir and bring back to the boil. Once boiling turn the stove down to low and leave to simmer for about 2 hours, stirring every now and then to make sure it does not stick to the pan. After 2 hours the onions should have cooked down and the liquid will have reduced so you're left with a nice sticky marmalade. If the marmalade still looks a little wet, just leave it on the stove for another half an hour to reduce more. Once ready, leave to cool then store in a container in the fridge. The red onion marmalade with keep in the fridge for 7 days. I like to serve my marmalade and cheese at room temperature.

The crackers could not be easier to make; in a large bowl mix all the dry ingredients. Add the milk and eggs and mix with your hands until you have a nice dough, this will take about 5 minutes to incorporate everything together and form the dough. Once you have it ready, wrap it with cling film and leave it in the fridge for at least 20 minutes to rest.

Preheat the oven to 180°c. Line a baking tray with greaseproof paper. Take out your dough and cut into four pieces, flour a work surface and roll out each quarter into 1mm thick sheets. Once rolled, place the sheet of dough onto the baking tray (I just use one baking tray and cook the dough in four batches). Place the tray into the oven and cook for 5 minutes, then open the oven door and flip the cracker over to brown the other side. After 5 minutes remove the tray and place the cracker onto a cake rack. Repeat the process a further three times until all your dough is cooked. Once the crackers are cool, snap them with your hands into pieces as big or small as you want and store in a biscuit tin until needed.

To Serve

Arrange your cheeses onto a plate or board, place the red onion marmalade into a bowl and serve with your homemade crackers.

SUMMER

It's Summer! Everyone is happy during this season; we have great weather and beautiful beaches so it's the season to holiday and relax – and thankfully our Great British produce is in abundance.

Some of the things that excite me most about summer are; the great heirloom tomatoes, cucumbers, beautiful salads and all the fresh fragrant herbs and fruit that are readily available.

Blueberries, raspberries, strawberries, plums; there are so many flavours and colours it's hard not to get excited.

The food in this season is so light, refreshing and healthy for us. It's a time of year to celebrate, so why not get out there and see what you can find.

I think it's the season where healthy becomes fun and we should all enjoy it together.

I've created a selection of dishes that will excite people, dishes that will let the ingredients do the talking.

HEIRLOOM TOMATO SALAD WITH SHEEP'S YOGHURT, DRIED BLACK OLIVE AND ROCKET

Ingredients | Serves 4-6

4 'Yellow Stuffer' tomatoes

4 'Black Russian' tomatoes

4 'Brandywine' tomatoes

4 'The Amateur' tomatoes

Olive oil

Sea salt

For the garnish

400g sheep's yoghurt

250g pitted black olives

Baby rocket leaves

Herbs and flowers

Heirloom tomatoes, also known as Heritage tomatoes, are varieties that have been in cultivation for 50 years or more. Although many Heirloom varieties have all but vanished due to the rise of the supermarket mass-produced tomatoes, there are farms in the UK still growing Heirloom tomatoes.

They're also experiencing a rise in popularity due to their stunning flavour and range of beautiful colours and are now available through most good markets and greengrocers.

For the dried black olive crumb make sure the olives are pitted and rinsed under cold water to remove any brine. Pat them dry and place on a metal tray. Place them in an oven at 40°c and leave them for 8-10 hours. I put these in the oven before I go to sleep at night and remove them the next day. The olives will dry out completely removing all their moisture. Once dried, leave to cool for a few hours out of the oven; don't chop them straight away warm because this could make an olive paste. Once cool, chop the olives with a knife until they look like an olive crumb. Store in a dry place until needed.

The beauty of this salad is the simplicity of the dish. We are celebrating some great produce here so there is no need to complicate it. The flavour of the tomatoes are incredible so a little olive oil and sea salt is all that is needed to season them. Take your mixed variety of tomatoes and cut them into pieces.

If you have big tomatoes, quarter them, a smaller one cut in half and if you have tiny ones just leave them whole. About six pieces of tomato per person is plenty for a starter. Place all your cut tomatoes in a bowl, season with some sea salt and dress with a good quality olive oil and mix gently with your hands.

To Serve

Take your sheep's yoghurt out of the fridge and place a tablespoon full on the side of each plate then with a spoon swipe the yoghurt around one side of the plate. Take the olive crumb and sprinkle over the yoghurt and around the plate. Divide the tomatoes evenly between the plates and garnish the salad with some rocket leaves, edible flowers and baby herbs. The colours on the plate are stunning and I can promise you it tastes even better than it looks.

SUMMER GARDEN VEGETABLE SALAD

This is a great salad that is visually stunning and will wow your friends. A simple dish that looks like a garden, the vegetables should look as if they are growing out of the soil; it's a real conversation starter to the meal. I have suggested five types of vegetables in this recipe but the beauty of this dish is that you can make it using as many different seasonal vegetables as you like.

Ingredients | Serves 6

For the vegetable garden

1 head broccoli

6 baby carrots

6 new potatoes

6 radishes

12 runner beans

For the soil

250g pitted black olives

50g peeled hazelnuts

For the dipping sauce

3 free range egg yolks

300ml virgin olive oil (approximately)

1 teaspoon white wine vinegar

Sea salt and pepper

½ lemon, juiced

30g chopped gherkins

30g capers

½ bunch tarragon, leaves removed and finely chopped

½ bunch parsley, finely chopped

4 anchovy fillets (optional)

For the sauce take a tall jug and place the egg yolks, white wine vinegar and lemon juice inside. Take a stick blender and blitz for a minute; after a minute very slowly add the olive oil blitzing constantly and the egg will slowly emulsify with the oil forming a mayonnaise, you'll need approximately 300ml of oil. The mayonnaise will thicken very quickly and may not require all the oil. Once the mayonnaise thickens add the gherkins, capers, anchovies, parsley and tarragon and blend together for one minute. Season with sea salt and pepper then tip the sauce into a container and chill until needed. This sauce will create the under layer of the salad, a nice green herby mayonaisse perfect for the vegetables.

For the soil, make sure the olives are pitted and rinsed under cold water to remove any brine. Pat them dry and place on a metal tray. Place them in an oven at 40°c and leave them for 8-10 hours. I put these in the oven before I go to sleep and remove them the next day. The olives will dry out completely removing all their moisture. Once dried, leave to cool for a few hours out of the oven. Don't chop them straight away warm because this could end up as an olive paste. Once cool chop the olives with a knife until they look like an olive crumb. In another metal tray take the hazelnuts and toast them gently under a grill until golden brown. Once golden, put them in a tea towel and with a rolling pin bash them to break them into a hazelnut crumb. Once broken add them to the olive crumb and mix together. Now the soil is ready. Store in a dry place until needed.

Now it's time to prepare the vegetables for the salad. With the broccoli remove the florets with a knife leaving a little stalk. Peel the baby carrots leaving the little green stalk out the top and remove the bottoms of the runner beans. In a pan of boiling lightly salted water cook the vegetables separately until tender then plunge into ice water to stop them cooking and ensure they keep their vibrant colour. Place the new potatoes in a pan of cold water with a pinch of sea salt and bring to the boil, cooking until tender. Cool under cold water. The radishes are best served raw so give them a good wash in a bowl of cold water. Take a tray, place a cloth on the tray and place all the prepared vegetables on the cloth to drain any excess water. This dish is served cold so can be made in advance and constructed last minute.

To Serve

In a serving dish spoon a layer of the sauce into the bottom and level it out with the back of your spoon. Sprinkle over the olive and nut soil to cover the sauce, take your vegetables and gently push them into the soil creating the vegetable patch. Place in the middle of the table and let everyone use their fingers to pull out and eat the vegetables.

LETTUCE GAZPACHO

Gazpacho is a chilled/cold soup normally made with tomatoes but my lettuce version is vibrant, colourful, refreshing and perfect on a hot summer's day.

Ingredients | Serves 6

2 green peppers

1 cucumber

1 fennel bulb

1 banana shallot, diced

1 garlic clove, crushed

3 large cos (romaine or gem) lettuce, roughly chopped

1 bunch chervil, roughly chopped

1 pint still cold mineral mater

3 tablespoons white wine vinegar

Sea salt and white pepper

100g mayonnaise

For the garnish

100g crème fraîche

This is such a simple starter to make and it's so tasty and fresh. Begin by preparing all the ingredients for the gazpacho; everything can be cut roughly as we will be blending it into a soup. Cut around the green peppers and discard the centre and stalk, dice the flesh roughly and cut the cucumber into a rough dice and chop the chervil. If you don't have chervil any other soft green herbs will work. Peel and dice the shallot, peel and crush the garlic with the back of a knife. For the fennel remove the bottom part then cut it in half down the middle. Remove the hard stalk with a knife and roughly chop the bulb, discard the root and any tough outer parts of the fennel bulb. If there are any fennel herbs on the bulb chop them and keep them with the diced fennel. Take the cos lettuce and cut in half, remove the root and remove any damaged outer leaves then roughly chop the lettuce. Place all the chopped ingredients into a food processor, season with some sea salt and white pepper then add the cold water and white wine vinegar. Blend all the ingredients together for 5 minutes, then add the mayonnaise and blend for a further 2 minutes. Pass the soup through a fine sieve using a spoon to push through all the juice. Tip the strained soup into a container and chill until needed.

To Serve

Take the chilled soup out of the fridge, pour into soup bowls and serve. Place a spoon of crème fraîche in the middle of each bowl for a nice creamy finish.

CURED AND CONFIT SALMON, CUCUMBER, DILL AND A HORSERADISH CREAM

This is a stunning dish which is perfect for a warm summer's evening. The salmon simply melts in the mouth; it's refreshing to eat and the colours on the plate are beautiful. For me, this is the perfect start to any meal.

Ingredients | Serves 6

For the confit salmon

6 x 150g fillets of organic salmon, skinned

60g caster sugar

40g Maldon sea salt

1 star anise

5 peppercorns

Olive oil (enough to cover the fish)

For the horseradish cream

90g horseradish sauce

400ml double cream

½ lemon

Salt and pepper

To garnish

1 cucumber

1 bunch dill

Loaf rye bread

This dish requires the freshest salmon you can find; start by taking the skin and any pin bones off and then cut into 150g portions. In a bowl, mix the caster sugar, sea salt, star anise and peppercorns together. Dry the salmon with a cloth, place half the salt/sugar mix on a tray, lay the salmon on top then cover with the remaining mix. Leave to cure for 5 hours. After curing remove the salmon and wash under cold water to remove all the sugar/salt mixture. Pat dry and place the salmon into a deep tray. Cover with olive oil, making sure it's fully submerged to retain the colour of the fish. Place the tray into an oven at 40°c and cook for 40 minutes. By cooking the salmon at such a low temperature it will give it the same texture and delicate flavour throughout as well as keeping its vivid orange colour. When cooked, the salmon will still appear raw to the eye but it will melt in the mouth. If your oven does not go as low as 40°c then you can place the tray on a stove top and monitor the temperature with a thermometer. After 40 minutes carefully remove the salmon from the oil, place in a plastic container, cover with some of the oil and store in the fridge until needed. The salmon will last for 4 days, as long as it's submerged in olive oil.

Take the cucumber, peel it and slice it into one to two inch pieces. With an apple corer remove the centre of the cucumber, place the pieces into a tub and freeze them overnight, discarding the centre pieces. The next day, take the tub out of the freezer and run it under cold water in order to defrost the cucumber. By shocking the cucumber this way it will soften and give it an almost cooked texture and it will go bright green in colour. Once defrosted, dry on a paper towel and pat dry, chill until needed.

For the horseradish cream, add the horseradish sauce and double cream to a bowl, squeeze in half a lemon, season with sea salt and pepper and whisk until slightly thickened. Don't over whip the cream; we want it light and smooth.

To Serve

Take the salmon out of the fridge, remove from the oil and place onto a tray with a cloth to drain off the excess oil. Once drained place a piece of salmon on each plate alongside a piece of cucumber. Fill the cucumber pieces with some horseradish cream as well as serving some extra of the cream on the plate. Take the dill and place some sprigs over the plate. Slice the rye bread and serve alongside the salmon.

We actually get the BBQ element of this dish by using a blow torch; when the flame touches the fresh mackerel skin it gives the fish this lovely charred flavour. The Japanese mayonnaise is very simple to make; it was a recipe I picked up on my travels and complements this dish very well.

BBQ MACKEREL, RADISH, GRILLED BABY GEM LETTUCE AND JAPANESE MAYONNAISE

Ingredients | Serves 6

6 mackerel fillets, pin bones removed

4 little gem lettuces

2 bunches baby garden radishes

Rapeseed oil

For the Japanese mayonnaise

3 free range egg yolks

300ml rapeseed oil (approximately)

6 tablespoons rice wine vinegar

Sea salt and pepper

Specialist equipment

Blow torch

For the Japanese mayonnaise take a tall jug and place the egg yolks and rice wine vinegar in the jug. Take a stick blender and blitz for a minute, then very slowly add the rapeseed oil, blitzing constantly and the egg will slowly emulsify with the oil forming a mayonnaise. Expect to use about 300ml of oil, although the mayonnaise will thicken very quickly and may not require all the oil. If the mayonnaise is too thick, add some more rice wine vinegar to thin it down slightly. Once it's the right consistency, season with salt and pepper and chill until needed.

Season the mackerel with sea salt and pepper then place the fillets flesh side down onto a lightly oiled tray. Rub some rapeseed oil onto the skin of the mackerel and with a blow torch begin to crisp the skin; just keep moving the flame up and down the fillets until you have a nice charred skin, this will take some time so be patient and make sure the flame is not set too high to allow the skin to get an even colour all over. If you don't have a blow torch then you can always cook the mackerel skin side down on a BBQ or place it under the grill; I really like the charred

flavour of the fish when the flame touches the skin. Once you have an even char leave on the tray until needed – the flesh will be slightly pink which is how I like it – but if you would like the fish cooked more just pop it into an oven for a few minutes to cook through.

For the lettuce, cut each one into quarters, season with sea salt and pepper and rub with rapeseed oil. Take the blow torch and char the outsides of the lettuce, this will take a few minutes. When all the quarters have a nice charred outside, set aside until ready to serve.

To Serve

Take the radishes and give them a good wash, either leave them whole or slice them depending on size and place a few on each plate. Radish is lovely raw and gives the dish some nice texture. Place a fillet of fish onto the plate, a few pieces of the lettuce and a dollop of the mayonnaise. This dish can be served warm or cold and is perfect on a summer evening.

HONEY GLAZED DUCK BREAST, PAK CHOI, ROAST PEACH AND DUCK SAUCE

Ingredients | Serves 6

6 duck breasts

100g clear honey

Salt and pepper

For the duck sauce

50ml port

Duck juices

500ml game stock (page 123)

½ lemon

For the garnish

3 peaches

½ bunch of lemon thyme

6 small pak choi

butter

olive oil

This is a really simple dish using some fantastic produce; the fruit with the duck works really well and helps cut through the richness of the meat. You finish this dish feeling really satisfied, it's a real favourite of mine with flavours that just work.

Start by cooking off the duck breasts. I like to serve my duck pink, this way it will stay tender, juicy and full of flavour. Start by placing a large deep frying pan over a medium heat. Take your duck breasts and season both sides with sea salt and pepper, then place the breast skin side down into the dry pan whilst it's still cold (no oil is needed as the fat will render out of the duck as it heats up). Cook gently for approximately 6 minutes, the fat will render out of the skin and the skin will begin to crisp. Spoon out any fat from the pan and turn over each breast and cook for a further 4 minutes, then squeeze the honey over the skin of the breasts, flip them over so the skin side is back down and caramelise for 1 minute. Remove the duck breasts from the pan and rest for 10 minutes on a tray, this will relax the meat leaving you with a perfectly cooked, juicy piece of meat.

Once the duck has been removed tip away the excess fat then place the pan back on the heat and turn it to high, add the port straight away and using a wooden spoon, scrape all the bits off the pan. Reduce the port by half then add the game stock, bring to a simmer, add a squeeze of lemon juice and pass through a fine sieve into a jug.

Take a sharp knife and run it through the middle of the peaches, when you hit the stone run the knife around it then pull the peaches carefully in half and remove each stone. Drizzle some olive oil over a roasting tray then with some paper towels rub the oil evenly over the tray. Pick the lemon thyme leaves, sprinkle into the tray then season with sea salt and pepper. Place each peach half into the tray flesh side down, then put the tray into a preheated oven at 180°c and roast for approximately 10 minutes.

Trim off the bottom of each pak choi then slice them in half from top to bottom. Place a large frying pan on the stove over a medium heat and add a knob off butter and a tablespoon of olive oil. Add the pak choi flat side down and cook for 2 minutes, turn over, season with sea salt and pepper and cook for a further minute. Once cooked, remove from the pan and place on a tray with a paper towel to soak up any excess moisture.

To Serve

Cut each duck breast in half lengthways to expose the pink flesh, then season the flesh with some sea salt. Place onto the plate, garnish with two pieces of pak choi and half a peach, drizzle over the sauce and serve.

FISH AND CHIPS: BEER BATTERED COD CHEEK, CRISPY FRIES, TARTARE SAUCE AND CRUSHED PEAS

Fish and Chips is the nation's most loved dish; it's a real classic and I think done properly it can be a stunning dish. I even won the 2011 Pub Chef Awards thanks to my fish and chips, it's a real crowd pleaser.

Ingredients | Serves 6

25 cod cheeks (about 20g each or 6 x 150g fillets of pollack or cod)

Plain flour for dusting

For the tartare sauce

3 free range egg yolks

350ml virgin olive oil (approximately)

1 teaspoon white wine vinegar

Sea salt and pepper

½ lemon, juiced

½ bunch parsley

3 tablespoons capers, drained

3 large gherkins, roughly diced

For the chips

6 large Maris Piper potatoes

Vegetable oil, for frying

For the beer batter

150ml beer

150ml sparkling water

350g self-raising flour

20g cornflour

Pinch sea salt

For the crushed peas

300g frozen peas

20g butter

1 shallot, finely diced

1 lemon, to garnish

For the fish I think cod cheeks are a real treat and create a little bit of conversation around the table. Speak to your local fishmonger and they will be happy to help but if all else fails, 150g per portion of a nice white fish such as pollack or cod will do the job nicely.

To start the tartare sauce take a tall jug and place the egg yolks, white wine vinegar and lemon juice inside. Take a stick blender and blitz for a minute, then very slowly add the olive oil blitzing constantly and the egg will slowly emulsify with the oil forming a mayonnaise. The mayonnaise will thicken very quickly and may not require all the oil. Once the mayonnaise thickens add the gherkins, capers, parsley and season with black pepper, blitz for a minute until everything is mixed. If it is too thick, add two tablespoons of cold water and blitz for 30 seconds to thin it down slightly. Tip into a container and chill until needed.

Next are the chips. They can be made in advance and re-cooked when needed. To start, peel and cut the potatoes into 2cm thick Jenga style chips. Once cut, place them in a bowl and run them under cold water for 5 minutes, this will remove the starch. Then place the chips into a pan of water and bring to a simmer for 3 minutes, strain into a colander and leave to cool for 10 minutes. Once cool, tip them out onto a kitchen cloth, you need to remove the excess water otherwise the oil will spit. Turn a table top fryer onto 130°c, place in the chips and fry for 5 minutes. Stick a knife into a chip, if it sticks into it with ease then they are ready.

Remove and leave to cool on a rack. It's at this stage you can place them into the fridge and leave them until you are ready to serve, up to 24 hours in advance.

For the beer batter, sift the flour and cornflour into a bowl then whisk in the beer and sparkling water until you have a nice thick, smooth batter. Season with a pinch of sea salt and set aside.

For the crushed peas simply place the peas into a food processor and blitz to crush (but not purée) them. You can do this from frozen. Finely dice the shallot and place in a saucepan with the butter. Sweat the shallot for a few minutes then add the peas from the processor. Season with sea salt and pepper then gently warm the peas through for a few minutes. You will have a lovely side of peas which are fresh in taste and still hold that lovely green colour.

To Serve

Have your fryer set at 180°c, place your fish into some seasoned flour and coat completely. Lift the fish out of the flour and tap off any excess, then place into the batter. Lift out the batter and carefully lower into the fryer oil. Fry the fish for about 3 minutes until golden and crisp. Once cooked, remove with a slotted spoon and drain on some kitchen paper. Add the chips, fry for 3-4 minutes until golden and crisp, drain onto some kitchen paper and sprinkle with sea salt. Place a piece of fish or 3-4 cod cheeks on a plate, add some crispy fries and serve with a wedge of lemon, some tartare sauce and a side of warm crushed peas. It really is a stunning dish.

BUTTER POACHED POLLACK, MARSH SAMPHIRE, MUSSELS AND A BUTTER SAUCE

I love poaching the fish gently in clarified butter like this, the fish stays so moist and really takes on some of those buttery flavours to just melt in the mouth. It's a really indulgent way to cook fish but fear not if you're on a health kick – simply grill the fish with a little olive oil.

Ingredients | Serves 6

6 x 150g fillets pollack or cod

1 litre clarified butter/2kg unsalted butter

For the butter sauce

4 shallots, peeled and roughly chopped

4 sprigs thyme

1 bay leaf

250ml white wine

200g diced cold butter

½ lemon

Sea salt and pepper

For the mussels

1kg live mussels, cleaned

100ml white wine

1 shallot, peeled and diced

1 clove of garlic, peeled and chopped

Sea salt and pepper

Olive oil

For the garnish

250g samphire, trimmed and washed

Clarified butter is a butter where all the milk solids have been removed leaving you with a pure yellow butter that can be heated to higher temperatures without burning; the taste is so much purer. To clarify the butter place all the butter in a heavy based saucepan and place over a low heat. Let the butter gently melt, this may take some time and once all the butter has melted turn off the heat and leave to settle for 15 minutes. The butter will separate from the milk solids so you will be left with pure yellow butter on the top of the pan and the white solids at the bottom. The next step is very important. Firstly, using a tablespoon, remove any impurities that may be on the top of the butter. Once you have done this take a ladle and very carefully move the butter bit by bit into another pan without disturbing the milk solids at the bottom. Transfer all the butter, then discard the white milk solids left in the bottom of the pan. Set aside in a deep saucepan until needed.

To make the butter sauce place the shallots, sprigs of thyme, bay leaf and white wine into a saucepan and place on the stove over a high heat. Bring to the boil and reduce by three quarters. Once reduced, take the pan off the heat and season with sea salt and pepper. Take a whisk and add your butter cube by cube, whisking constantly until all of the butter has emulsified into the sauce. Once the butter is whisked into the sauce it will thicken, make sure this is done off the heat otherwise the sauce will split, the residual heat in the pan will be enough to melt the butter. Strain through a sieve and discard the shallots, bay leaf and thyme, add a squeeze of lemon juice to the sauce and you will be left with a slightly thick, shiny butter sauce.

Check that all your mussels are closed, if any are open discard them.

Take a heavy based saucepan, add a splash of olive oil and place over a high heat. Add the garlic and shallot and fry for 2 minutes. Just as the shallots begin to colour, add the mussels, sea salt, pepper and white wine, place a lid on the pan and cook for 4 minutes on high until all the mussels have opened. Once opened, tip the mussels into a colander, if any haven't opened discard them. With the open mussels take them out of the shells and put the mussel meat into the butter sauce and mix together.

Place a pan of water over a high heat, when boiling add the samphire and cook for 3 minutes. Once cooked strain the water away, drizzle some olive oil and black pepper over the samphire and place the lid back on to steam for a few minutes. No salt is needed as samphire is naturally salty.

Place the saucepan of clarified butter back onto a very low heat, with a thermometer try and monitor the temperature to about 68°c (no higher than 72°c) to gently poach the fish. Place the fillets of fish into the butter and poach for approximately 13 minutes. If the temperature gets too high just remove the pan from the heat. The fish will go slightly opaque and will be cooked perfectly with the most amazing texture and buttery taste. Once the fish is poached, remove carefully with a spatula and place on a tray with a cloth to remove any excess butter.

To Serve

Start by placing some samphire on to each plate, place a fillet of butter poached pollack on the samphire and spoon over the mussel butter sauce.

VANILLA BEAN PANNA COTTA WITH A CHILLED RASPBERRY AND LEMONGRASS SOUP

This is a beautiful summer dessert; the creamy panna cotta with the fragrant chilled raspberry and lemongrass soup really complement each other. It can be made well in advance and takes moments to put on the plate meaning you have more time to socialise and less time to worry about cooking.

Ingredients | Serves 6
For the panna cotta

2 vanilla pods

284ml double cream

200ml whole milk

2 gelatine leaves

50g caster sugar

For the raspberry and lemongrass soup

1½ litre water

310g caster sugar

3 lemongrass sticks

1kg raspberries

For the garnish

200g fresh raspberries

Both elements of this dessert require forward planning and need to be made at least 3 hours before serving but preferably make them the day before, which will give you less to worry about on the day of your meal.

Starting with the panna cotta take the gelatine leaves and soak them in cold water for 10 minutes until they soften. Pour the cream, milk and caster sugar into a heavy based saucepan and put on the stove over a medium heat. Whilst the cream mixture heats, cut open the vanilla pods and with the back of a knife remove all the seeds. Add the seeds and split vanilla pods to the cream mixture. When the cream begins to simmer turn off the heat, remove the soft gelatine from the water and add to the hot cream. Whisk in the pan for a few seconds to disperse the vanilla seeds and dissolve the gelatine. Leave to infuse for 15 minutes then discard the empty vanilla pods. Pour the panna cotta mixture into six dariole moulds or six ramekins, place in the fridge and chill until needed. They will take approximately 3 hours to set.

The raspberry and lemongrass soup can also be done in advance and will actually improve in flavour if left to infuse for 24 hours

as it will intensify the lemongrass flavour of the soup. Start by adding the water and sugar to a heavy based saucepan, place on a high heat and bring to the boil. Once at a rolling boil remove from the heat and add the raspberries. Using a stick blender and being careful, liquidise the raspberries in the liquid until you have no pieces of fruit left, then leave the mixture to cool for an hour. After 1 hour, strain the liquid through a fine sieve into a container. Using the back of a knife hit the lemongrass sticks to break and bruise them which will release their lovely fragrant flavour, then add to the raspberry soup and leave to infuse in the fridge until needed.

To Serve

Take the chilled raspberry soup and strain through a fine sieve into a jug to remove the lemongrass. Pour the soup into your serving bowls. Gently heat a pan of water on the stove; once hot take each panna cotta and gently lower the bottom of the dariole mould into the water, releasing the panna cotta from the mould. Using two fingers press on the side of the panna cotta and they will slide out of the moulds. Place in the bowl and garnish with a few fresh raspberries.

FROZEN AERATED MILK CHOCOLATE PARFAIT WITH FRESH CHERRIES

This is a really special dessert; a frozen aerated chocolate parfait is as light as air, melts in the mouth and tastes amazing. Have a go at using different chocolates; milk, dark or white chocolate all work fantastically.

Ingredients | Serves 6

For the parfait

210g milk, white or dark chocolate

150g double cream

150g egg whites

3 tablespoons vegetable oil

For the garnish

250g fresh cherries

10g icing sugar

Specialist equipment

Thermo whip, 3 cream chargers

This dessert requires a little effort but has the 'wow' factor. Unfortunately it can only be made with a thermo whip so I strongly suggest getting one so you can try this out for yourself. They are sold in all good kitchen shops and are available online. A thermo whip which holds ½ litre is perfect for this recipe.

To make the parfait, pour the double cream into a saucepan and put on the stove over a low heat. Put whichever flavour chocolate you choose into a bowl and add three tablespoons of vegetable oil, then leave to one side. When the cream begins to simmer take the pan off the heat and pour it over the chocolate. With a wooden spoon mix the mixture until the chocolate has melted and mixed with the cream. Once mixed, pour the mixture into the thermo whip canister. Weigh out the egg whites and then pour into the canister with the cream, chocolate and vegetable oil. Screw on the lid and shake well for 1 minute. Once shaken, charge with 1 cream charger and shake for 2 minutes as hard as you can. Remove the charger and charge again, shaking hard for another 2 minutes. Once complete, take the empty charge out and place the canister somewhere warm for 15 minutes. The reason for charging and shaking it so much is so we can create as many air bubbles as possible to aerate the chocolate. Whilst we leave the chocolate, take a large terrine mould or a two litre plastic container and line it with cling film. Use three layers so it will be easier to pull out of the mould when frozen. Just one layer of cling film could tear when you try and remove the parfait. Place the lined terrine mould in the freezer.

After 15 minutes take the thermo whip, place a cloth over the nozzle and release the gas. Once released, charge the thermo whip with a third charger and shake for 2 minutes. Remove the container from the freezer and squeeze the thermo whip handle aiming the nozzle into the container or terrine mould until all the chocolate has been released. The chocolate will come out of the canister full of air and really frothy. Once the container is full to the top with the aerated chocolate, place in the freezer and leave for a minimum of 24 hours.

Take the cherries and remove the pips by tearing them in half. Place all the halves in a bowl and dust with the icing sugar, mix and leave for 10 minutes. Some of the juices will run out of the cherries, leaving them with a lovely glaze.

To Serve

Take the parfait out of the freezer, remove from the container and remove the cling film. If you are serving one type of chocolate cut the parfait into 3cm thick pieces and place on the plate. If you have made different flavours (I have made white, dark and milk chocolate parfait), cut the parfaits into chunks and arrange around each plate. You will feel how light the parfait is and see the air bubbles inside the chocolate. Take the cherries and mix in their own juices. Scatter the cherries over each plate and serve straight away.

STRAWBERRIES AND CREAM: VANILLA CREAM, STRAWBERRY JELLY AND FRESH STRAWBERRIES

Ingredients | Serves 6

For the jelly

500g fresh strawberries, quartered

600ml water

250g caster sugar

200ml white wine

11 gelatine leaves

For the cream

500ml double cream

1 vanilla pod, split

5g icing sugar

For the garnish

250g fresh strawberries

10g icing sugar

It wouldn't be summer without strawberries and cream. Here is my version of this classic dessert to celebrate the great British strawberry.

The jelly can be made in advance; if you are making it the same day you plan to serve it, make sure you give the jelly a minimum of 2 hours to set in the fridge. To make the jelly start by soaking the gelatine and placing it in a bowl of cold water. It will become soft after about 5 minutes. Meanwhile take a heavy based saucepan and add the sugar and water. Place over a high heat and bring to the boil, leave for 1 minute to dissolve the sugar then remove the pan from the heat. Add the white wine, fresh strawberries and take the softened gelatine out the water and add to the pan. Using a stick blender blend everything together for 5 minutes until the strawberries have been completely puréed. Once you have done this, leave the pan on the side for 30 minutes to infuse. Then pass the liquid through a fine sieve into a deep tray and set in the fridge for a minimum of 2 hours.

For the vanilla cream add the double cream to a mixing bowl, cut the vanilla pod down the middle top to bottom and using the back of a knife remove all the vanilla seeds by running the knife down each inside half of the vanilla pod. Add the seeds to the cream along with the icing sugar and whip until you have soft peaks. Add the whipped cream to a piping bag and chill until needed.

With the remaining 500g of fresh strawberries cut them into a small dice and place in a bowl, dust with the icing sugar and mix. Set aside until needed.

To Serve

Remove the jelly from the fridge. With a small circular cutter, cut six discs of jelly about 8cm in diameter. With a second cutter about 4cm in diameter, cut another six discs. If you do not have a circular cutter you could cut the jelly into squares or any shape you want.

Place a large round of the jelly in the centre of each plate then top with a smaller round, take the whipped cream and pipe around the jelly. Top with the freshly diced strawberries and serve.

BERRIES AND SNOW:
FRESH SUMMER BERRIES
WITH FROZEN YOGHURT

This is a perfect dessert on a hot summer's evening. It is such a simple dish which basically involves frozen yoghurt and fresh fruit; any summer fruits will work with this and the frozen yoghurt is shaved with a spoon to resemble snowflakes.

This couldn't be easier. To make the snow put both yoghurts, water, lemon juice and sugar in a bowl and whisk for a few minutes to incorporate all of the ingredients together. Once mixed, pour into a sealed plastic container and freeze. Leave for 24 hours. The next day remove from the freezer and with a spoon begin to scrape the yoghurt into another plastic container. This will give you a snow-like texture; it might take a while but once you have scraped it into snow, re-freeze in another container until desired.

Place all the fruit into a bowl cutting the strawberries in half and leaving the other berries whole. Add the icing sugar and mix, the icing sugar will release the juices from the fruit. Leave the fruit for a few minutes to steep in their own juices.

To Serve

Place the mixed fruit in the centre of each plate, remove the frozen yoghurt and sprinkle over the berries. Serve straight away.

The frozen yoghurt will sit in the freezer happily for 2 months so I like to have it to hand as it makes a great snack on a hot afternoon or even on some fresh fruit for breakfast.

Ingredients | Serves 6
For the frozen yoghurt (snow)
300ml water
80g caster sugar
300g sheep's yoghurt
300g cow's yoghurt
15g lemon juice
For the berries
1 punnet blueberries
1 punnet raspberries
1 punnet strawberries
1 punnet blackberries
1 tablespoon icing sugar

AUTUMN

I love autumn; the leaves are beginning to fall, the countryside begins to change and along with it we get a whole new larder of ingredients.

The flavours are a lot bolder, stronger and earthier. In the forest, game is upon us; that means duck, rabbit, pheasant and guinea fowl, while we also have nuts, mushrooms and kale.

Meanwhile, we have fantastic oysters and other shellfish along the coast so it's a great time to celebrate British produce.

The flavours in this season need to be kept simple; they are so strong we can let the produce do the talking, making it a real season to celebrate.

I've created dishes with real bold flavours using some of the best produce we have to offer, great tasting food that delivers that will impress your friends.

CANAPÉS: SEED MERINGUES AND OAT BISCUITS WITH SOUR CREAM, HERBS AND FLOWERS

These little canapés are the perfect snack to start a meal; they are delicious, perfect for vegetarians, pack a real punch in flavour, look beautiful and are really healthy.

Ingredients | Serves 6-8 For the seed meringues	For the oat crackers	To garnish
500g egg whites	200g oats	200g sour cream
35g caster sugar	1½ litres water	1 lemon, zest
20g table salt	150g butter	10g red amaranth
140g plain flour	7g table salt	10g dill sprigs
40g poppy seeds	olive oil	10g edible flowers
40g sesame seeds		10g borage leaves
40g pumpkin seeds		10g chives

These little canapés might look simple but they are in fact fairly complex. Each element is time consuming but firstly – it's worth the effort – and secondly they can be made the day before which means on the day of your meal you can spend more time socialising and less time in the kitchen.

Before we go on I would like to talk about the herbs and flowers. These are what will sit on the canapés as a garnish so it's important to get some herbs that taste good and also some flowers that are colourful and look good. I have given a few ideas of some herbs but please visit your local greengrocer and see what's available; micro herbs are very easy to get hold of now and the varieties are endless.

Starting with the seed meringues take a pestle and mortar, grind the poppy seeds, sesame seeds and pumpkin seeds until completely crushed into a crumb. You could also do this in a food processor. In a large mixing bowl whisk the egg whites until they have reached a soft peak. Once whipped add the sifted flour, salt, sugar and seeds to the egg whites and fold all the ingredients together with a spoon. Place a non-stick baking mat onto a baking tray, add a drizzle of olive oil and wipe over with some paper towel. Using a tablespoon spoon all the mix on to a tray. Once you have done this, tap the tray on the side to level out. Place into a preheated oven at 160°c and bake for 8 minutes. Remove the tray and using a circular cutter (approximately 3cm in diameter) start cutting discs. Remove all the excess meringue leaving you with just the discs, this will be very easy. Place the tray back into the oven and bake the discs for a further 8 minutes. Remove and cool. Tip the discs into a container and store in a dark, dry place.

The oat crackers are very simple but time consuming. In a heavy based saucepan add the oats, water, butter and salt and place on a low to medium heat, we just want to barely simmer the oats in the pan. Cook the oats on the stove for 1½ hours, stirring often, making sure they don't stick to the pan. After 1½ hours you will be left with a thick consistency and the oats will be tender. Take a non-stick baking mat and place it onto a baking tray, brush with oil then tip out the oats. Using a palette knife spread the oats out covering the whole tray and spread them a few millimetres thick keeping the oats as one sheet. Place into a preheated oven at 160°c and cook for 50 minutes. After 50 minutes, reduce the oven's temperature to 140°c and cook for a further 20 minutes. Remove from the oven, flip over the large oat sheet, place back into the oven and cook for a further 20 minutes. Once cooked, remove from the oven and allow to cool. Break the oat cracker into pieces as big or small as you like, place into a container and store in a dark, dry place.

To Serve

Place your pieces of oat crackers and seed meringues onto a tray, or enough for a few pieces per person. Top each piece with a little sour cream and grate the lemon zest over the canapés. Take your selection of herbs and flowers, chop and tear the herbs into little pieces and arrange a few of each type over each canapé. Take each canapé and place on a plate and serve straight away. The contrast between the crunchy oats and soft meringue is great.

CRISPY PIGS' EARS WITH A BRAMLEY APPLE SAUCE

Pigs' ears are a very underused part of the pig but served crispy like this they make the ultimate little starter; after all, everyone loves pork and apple.

Your butcher will be able to supply you with pigs' ears. With some sharp scissors cut out and discard the inner ridge section of the ear leaving the outer ear intact. Place the ears into a heavy based saucepan with the carrots, celery, white onion, parsley stalks and peppercorns. Cover with cold water and place the pan on the stove and simmer for 5 hours. After this time, remove the pigs' ears from the water and leave to cool. Pat completely dry, then with a sharp knife, slice the ears as thinly as possible. Place the thin slices into a bowl and dust with some plain flour, coating evenly. In a table top fryer or a heavy based saucepan heat vegetable oil to 180°c. Shake off any excess flour and fry the ears until golden brown. Once cooked, drain them onto some kitchen cloth and season with sea salt.

To make the apple sauce, peel and remove the core from each apple, cut each apple into quarters, then cut each quarter into 1cm pieces. Place all the diced apple into a heavy based pan with the sugar, water, butter and juice of one lemon, place on the stove and simmer for 15 minutes until all the apple has broken down into a chunky purée.

To Serve

Pour the apple sauce into a serving pot and pile the crispy pigs' ears next to it, place in the middle of the table and let everyone dive in.

Ingredients | Serves 4-6

6 pigs' ears

1 white onion, peeled and chopped

1 carrot, chopped

1 stick celery, chopped

5 peppercorns

A few parsley stalks

Sea salt

Plain flour for dusting

Vegetable oil, for frying

For the bramley apple sauce

5 bramley apples

50ml water

100g caster sugar

25g butter

1 lemon, juiced

A BROTH OF AUTUMN MUSHROOMS AND SOY

If you could taste autumn this would be it. The broth has such a depth of flavour and leaves you with this warm happy feeling. If you close your eyes and eat this it would almost feel like you're walking through the forest on a cool autumn evening. The perfect starter for the season.

Ingredients | Serves 6

For the mushroom broth

20ml olive oil

45g butter

500g button mushrooms

2 litres white chicken stock, optional (page 123)

1 litre water

200g dried cep or wild mushrooms

150ml dark soy sauce (approximately)

1 stick celery, chopped

1 carrot, peeled and chopped

1 bulb garlic, split in half

1 white onion, peeled and diced

1 leek, diced

½ bunch thyme

½ bunch rosemary

To garnish

6 button mushrooms, sliced

This recipe uses chicken stock which adds another layer of depth to the broth and gives the dish a real meatiness but if you are a vegetarian, then simply substitute the chicken stock for water and you'll have an equally delicious version.

Make sure you plan ahead with this dish; the broth needs a good 12 hours to infuse so make this the day before you need it.

Start by slicing the button mushrooms. Take a large heavy based saucepan and place on a high heat, add the olive oil and butter. When the butter melts add the sliced button mushrooms and fry until golden. Once golden, add the celery, carrot, white onion, garlic, leek, thyme and rosemary and fry for a further 5 minutes. Add the water, chicken stock and dried mushroom to the pan, give it a good stir and simmer for 45 minutes. Turn off the heat and leave to cool then tip the mix into a container and chill in the fridge overnight, this will give the broth a deeper flavour by allowing everything to infuse together.

The next day, take the broth out of the fridge and tip back into a pan, bring it back up to a gentle simmer to make it easier to strain. Strain the broth into another pan through a fine sieve and use a spoon to squeeze as much liquid as you can through. Season the broth with the soy sauce. Have a taste and if it needs more seasoning add more soy sauce; this is our salty aspect and adds real depth to the broth.

To Serve

Take your raw button mushrooms, make sure they are clean, with a knife slice them as thinly as possible. Divide the sliced mushrooms amongst the bowls, pour the warm broth into a tea pot, place each bowl in front of your guests and pour the warm broth over the raw mushrooms at the table.

DEEP FRIED ROCK OYSTER IN PANKO BREADCRUMBS, DUCK HAM AND APPLE

This is a real crowd pleaser. Deep frying oysters in crispy breadcrumbs is a great way to serve them and even people who normally wouldn't eat raw oysters will love them cooked. It changes the texture completely and they are delicious. Match that with your own cured duck ham and you have a real winner.

Ingredients | Serves 6

For the oysters

18 rock oysters

100g plain flour

100g panko breadcrumbs

3 whole eggs, beaten

Vegetable oil for deep frying

Specialist Equipment

Muslin cloth

For the duck ham

1 large duck breast (300g)

75g coarse sea salt

10 black peppercorns, crushed

5 sprigs fresh thyme leafs

25g caster sugar

To garnish

2 Cox's apples

750g coarse sea salt (This can be reused)

Making the duck ham

The duck ham is an optional extra; the surf and turf element of this dish really works well but bear in mind, forward planning is essential as it will take 10 days to cure the duck breast. If you do not want to attempt this you can substitute the duck ham for a good quality salami or any other cured meat from a deli. Start by removing half the fat off the duck breast with a knife then in a bowl mix together the salt, pepper, thyme and sugar. In a small plastic container place a layer of the salt mixture on the bottom, put the duck breast on the salt mix then cover the breast with the remaining salt mixture. The thyme is very important in this recipe because as well as adding flavour it contains antibacterial agents that will protect the meat from contamination as it cures. Cover the container with cling film and place in the fridge for 24 hours. After 24 hours remove the duck breast from the cure and wash it under cold running water to remove all the salt mix, pat dry with kitchen towel and wrap it in muslin cloth. Tie some string around the end and hang the duck breast in the fridge for 10 days. It is important that the air can circulate freely around the meat so make sure you clear some space in the fridge. After 10 days remove the duck from the cloth and the beautifully cured duck ham is ready for eating.

Opening the oysters

We call this shucking. Hold the oyster flat side up and use a tea towel to protect your hands in case you slip when opening the oysters. Insert an oyster shucker or butter knife into the hinge of the oyster, ease the knife in gently then twist the knife to open the oyster. Discard the flat part of the shell and – using a spoon – carefully scrape the oyster into a bowl. Once you have done this to all the oysters, keep the meat in the fridge until needed and wash the curved part of the shells as we will use these later to serve the oysters in.

Just before you are ready to serve place the flour, beaten eggs and breadcrumbs in three separate bowls. Take the oysters out the fridge and place each one in the flour first, then the egg and finally the breadcrumbs. Make sure a decent layer of the crumbs stick to each oyster. Place the breaded oysters onto a clean tray ready for frying.

To Serve

Heat a table top fryer or deep saucepan with vegetable oil to 180°c. Whilst the oil is heating tip the coarse salt into a serving dish then place the cleaned oyster shells into the salt, which is there to stop all the shells from tipping over. Taking a sharp knife, thinly slice the apple then cut into matchsticks. Remove the duck breast from the fridge and thinly slice. Once the oil is hot, fry the oysters for 2 minutes then drain on kitchen paper to remove excess oil. Place a deep fried oyster into each oyster shell, top with a slice of duck ham and some apple then serve straight away.

RAINBOW TROUT WITH A WATERCRESS PURÉE, SHAVED FENNEL, GRILLED BABY LEEK AND TROUT ROE

This fish dish has a few components to it which all work together so well … cooking the trout in olive oil retains its beautiful colour and gives it a melt in the mouth texture. All the colours make it really pleasing to the eye… and I promise, it tastes even better.

Ingredients | Serves 4-6

4-6 fillets rainbow trout, 200-250g each

60g caster sugar

40g Maldon sea salt

1 star anise

5 peppercorns

220ml olive oil

For the watercress purée

100g baby spinach

500g watercress

300ml water

1 small potato

Salt and pepper

To garnish

100g trout roe

12 baby leeks

2 bulbs fennel

Olive oil

½ lemon

Specialist equipment

Blow torch

This dish requires the freshest rainbow trout; ask your fishmonger to pin bone, scale and cut the trout into 200-250g portions then cut each portion in half giving two 100g pieces of fish per person. In a bowl mix the caster sugar, sea salt, star anise and peppercorns together. Dry the trout with a cloth, place half the salt/sugar mix on a tray, lay the fish on top then cover with the remaining mix. Leave to cure for 5 hours. After 5 hours remove the trout and wash under cold water to remove all the sugar/salt mixture. Pat dry and place into a deep tray. Cover the trout with the olive oil, making sure the fillets are fully submerged to retain the colour of the fish. Place the tray into an oven at 40°c and cook for 40 minutes; by cooking the trout at such a low temperature it will give it the same texture and delicate flavour throughout as well as retain the vivid colour of the fish. Once cooked, the trout appears to be raw and when you eat it, the fish will melt in your mouth. If your oven does not go as low as 40°c, then you can place the tray on a stove top and monitor the temperature with a thermometer. After 40 minutes carefully remove the fish from the oil, place in a plastic container, cover with some of the oil and store in the fridge until needed. The trout will last for 3 days in the fridge submerged in olive oil.

For the watercress purée, take a small potato, peel, wash, cut into quarters and slice as thinly as possible so it cooks as quickly as possible. Place the potato and water into a heavy based saucepan and boil until the potato is soft, if sliced thinly this will only take 5 minutes. Pick the watercress and spinach leaves and place into a tall blender. Once cooked, pour over the soft potato and water and blend until smooth. Once smooth, place a bowl over ice and strain the purée through a sieve into the bowl allowing the ice underneath to cool the purée to keep its bright green colour. Season with sea salt and pepper.

Cut the tops and bottom off the fennel and remove the woody outer shell. Cut the fennel in half, remove the hard core and slice as thinly as possible on a mandolin. Place into a bowl of iced water for 5 minutes to shock and keep it fresh and bright. Once removed from the ice water, dress with a little olive oil and a squeeze of lemon.

Take a little off the top and bottom of the leek and cook on a grill for a few minutes on each side. The leeks are so small they don't require much cooking. Once soft place onto a plate and dress the leeks with some olive oil and sea salt whilst warm.

To Serve

Gently heat some purée and place on the bottom of each plate. Take the trout out of the oil and onto a metal tray and crisp the skin with a blow torch, placing two pieces on the purée. Garnish the dish with a few baby leeks, a few slices of raw fennel, some trout roe dressed with a little olive oil (optional) and a few baby herbs.

DOUBLE COOKED SHOULDER OF LAMB WITH HERITAGE CARROTS, RUNNER BEANS AND A LAMB SAUCE

This dish won at The Pub Chef of the Year Awards in London in 2009; a very proud moment for me and the first major award I won. The tender, melt in the mouth braised lamb with the rich lamb gravy made from the cooking stock is intense in flavour and delicious when served with these beautiful British vegetables. It's one of those dishes you will make again and again.

Ingredients | Serves 6
For the lamb

1 lamb shoulder boned and rolled, approximately 2kg

1 bottle red wine

Water to cover

2 carrots washed, peeled and roughly chopped

1 leek, washed and roughly chopped

1 white onion, peeled and roughly chopped

½ head celery, washed and roughly chopped

1 bulb garlic, split in half

½ bunch rosemary

½ bunch thyme

For the lamb gravy

The cooking liquor from the lamb

100ml tomato juice

½ lemon, juiced

To garnish

500g runner beans

1 bunch or 5 large heritage carrots

50g butter

Salt and pepper

This dish requires forward planning; to allow the lamb time to cook and set it really needs to be made the day before so it can set in the fridge for a minimum of 8 hours. This is why I think it's the perfect dinner party main course. All the work is done the day before which gives you more time to socialise and spend time with friends whilst also producing an amazingly tasty and good looking meal.

Start by cooking the lamb. In a large heavy based saucepan add a touch of olive oil and place over a high heat. Add the shoulder of lamb and seal the outside moving the shoulder around the pan to colour all sides. Then add the carrot, leek, onion, garlic, celery, thyme and rosemary and brown in the pan for a further 5 minutes. Now season with a touch of sea salt and black pepper then add the red wine to the pan. Top with water until the lamb is covered. Turn down the heat to medium once the lamb starts boiling and leave to simmer for 4½ hours. Once cooked, the lamb will be so tender it will just fall apart. Turn off the stove top and using some kitchen utensils very carefully remove the lamb from the liquid and place on a tray, leave to cool for 30 minutes or until you can manage it with your hands but do not let it cool completely. Once the meat isn't too hot remove the string and start to pull the meat apart; flake all off the meat and remove any fat from in and around the lamb. You can break the meat up as much as you want, just make sure all the fat is removed. Once you are left with just the tender meat, roll out cling film onto a board, take the lamb and place it along the middle of the cling film. Start to roll it and with the cling film still attached keep rolling the lamb six times until you have a long sausage shape about 8cm in diameter. Cut off the cling film roll then tie each end of the lamb sausage, place in the fridge to set over night.

For the lamb gravy strain the cooking liquid through a fine sieve into another pan; there will be so much flavour in this liquid that it will produce an amazing sauce. Place on the stove on a high heat and with a ladle remove any surface fat. Add the tomato juice and the juice of half a lemon, reduce by three-quarters until you have a thick lamb gravy that coats the back of a spoon. Season with black pepper and the gravy is ready.

To prepare the vegetables bring a pan of salted water to the boil, cut the runner beans diagonally and cook for a few minutes until tender. Peel and cut the carrots, leave any baby ones whole and cook until tender. Once the vegetables are cooked, heat the butter and coat the vegetables in the butter, season with sea salt and pepper.

To Serve

Preheat the oven to 180°c. Take the lamb from the fridge, slice the cylinder into 4-6 pieces, remove the cling film and place onto a roasting tray with a touch of oil. Put in the oven for 15 minutes, this is just to warm the lamb through, it will still keep the round shape. Add the selection of vegetables to each plate, place a piece of lamb next to them and pour over the gravy. When you put your fork into the lamb it will just fall apart and melt in the mouth.

WILD MUSHROOM RISOTTO, PICKLED MUSHROOM AND FRESH BLACK TRUFFLE

This is a real autumnal dish; hearty wild mushrooms, creamy risotto, lightly pickled mushrooms and indulgent truffle. This is a plate of food that will really make you feel good.

Ingredients | Serves 6

350g Arborio rice

For the mushroom sauce

100g dried cep mushrooms

200ml white wine

1½ litres of water

1 sprig thyme

1 white onion

3 cloves garlic

200ml double cream

For the pickled mushroom

100g enoki mushrooms

125ml water

200ml white wine vinegar

125g caster sugar

5 coriander seeds

To finish

100g fresh parmesan, grated

100g fresh truffle or white truffle oil

200g wild mushrooms, cleaned and sliced

25g butter

Small bunch of chives, chopped

Salt and pepper

Olive oil

This simple looking risotto is a little more time consuming than it looks but well worth it in the end. It is crammed full of earthy flavours and a real crowd pleaser. Preparation is the key with this dish and actually everything can be made either on the day of your dinner party or the day before, as all the elements are brought together at the last minute.

My way of cooking risotto is not exactly conventional but a lot easier and less hassle, and in my opinion gives the same result. Simply boil a large pan of water on the stove, add the rice to the water once boiling then cook for 7 minutes exactly. Strain the rice in a colander, cool it down under cold running water and once cool, store in the fridge until needed.

For the mushroom sauce, heat a tablespoon of olive oil in a heavy based saucepan over a high heat on the stove. Add the onion, garlic, thyme and dried mushrooms and brown for a few minutes. To this, add the white wine and reduce by half, then add the water and boil for 15 minutes. Add the double cream and simmer for 10 minutes more, turn off the heat and leave to infuse for 30 minutes. Strain the sauce through a fine sieve and chill until needed.

The pickled mushrooms are an optional garnish that bring another element to the dish. Simply add the water, sugar, coriander seeds and vinegar to a pan and bring to a boil. Boil for 5 minutes then turn off the heat and leave to infuse for 30 minutes. Meanwhile cut off the roots of the enoki mushrooms, discard and place the rest of the mushrooms in a container. Strain the pickling liquid through a fine sieve onto the mushrooms and store in the fridge for a minimum of 1 hour.

To Serve

In a heavy based saucepan heat a tablespoon of olive oil and the butter over a medium heat, add the wild mushrooms and sauté for 5 minutes. To this add the risotto rice, stir briefly, then add half the mushroom sauce. Stir and bring to a simmer, add the grated parmesan and season with sea salt and pepper. Keep adding more mushroom sauce until you have a creamy, dark mushroom risotto which is nice and loose and not stodgy; this will take about 10 minutes. Once you have a nice consistency, fold in the chopped chives and spoon into your serving bowls. Finish with a few of the pickled enoki mushrooms and slices of fresh truffle or a drizzle of white truffle oil.

FIVE SPICE DUCK BREAST WITH A CELERIAC PURÉE AND KALE

This is a really simple dish that works so well … the creaminess of the celeriac purée with the juicy duck breast and the buttered kale all come together in perfect harmony.

Ingredients | Serves 6
6 duck breasts

10g Chinese five spice

For the celeriac purée
1 celeriac

1 litre whole milk

500ml double cream

Sea salt and pepper

To garnish
150g kale, stalks removed

20g butter

Place the celeriac on a chopping board and using a sharp knife remove the top and bottom parts, which will stop it rolling around. Carefully run the knife around the edge of the celeriac to peel off the outer skin. Once you have done this, dice into roughly 1cm cubes and place in a heavy based saucepan with the milk and cream. Bring to the boil over a high heat; once boiling, reduce the heat and simmer until soft. Then liquidise in a blender or with a stick blender until smooth. If the purée is too thick add a touch more cream to loosen. Season with salt and pepper and keep aside until needed.

When cooking the duck breasts I like to serve my duck pink, this way it will stay tender, juicy and full of flavour. Take a large deep frying pan and place over a medium heat. Season both sides of your duck breasts with sea salt, pepper and Chinese five spice. Place the breast skin side down in the dry pan (no oil is needed as the fat will render out of the duck). Cook gently for 6 minutes; the fat will render out of the skin and it will begin to crisp. After 6 minutes, spoon out any fat from the pan and turn over each breast and cook for a further 4 minutes, then flip them back over so the skin side is back down, spooning any juices back over the meat. Remove the duck breasts from the pan and rest for 10 minutes on a tray. Tip any pan juices over the breasts; resting the duck for 10 minutes will relax the meat leaving you with a perfectly cooked, juicy piece of meat.

To Serve

Heat the butter in a frying pan over a medium heat until foaming, add the kale and gently cook in the butter for 2 minutes. Season with salt and pepper and set aside. Cut each duck breast in half lengthways, season the exposed flesh with sea salt and place on the plate. Spoon the celeriac purée next to the duck and add a pile of the buttered kale.

STICKY TOFFEE PUDDING WITH A STICKY TOFFEE SAUCE

This is the ultimate British dessert and I have had this recipe in my note book for as long as I can remember. It's never changed; a true great British classic.

Ingredients | Serves 10
For the toffee pudding

500g pitted dates, chopped

700ml water

125g melted butter

460g caster sugar

6 whole eggs

460g self-raising flour

1½ teaspoons bicarbonate of soda

For the toffee sauce

250g unsalted butter

225g demerara sugar

4 tablespoons black treacle

600ml double cream

This recipe makes at least 10 generous portions but don't fear, cling film any remaining and place in the freezer for up to 3 months; they make a great snack or quick dessert and children love them.

Starting with the sticky toffee pudding, place the chopped, pitted dates and water into a heavy based saucepan. Bring to the boil and simmer for 15 minutes to soften, after 15 minutes turn off the heat and leave them to cool slightly. Meanwhile, use an electric whisk on a high setting to beat together the sugar and eggs in a mixing bowl until pale in colour. Then turn down to low and add the sifted flour, melted butter, bicarbonate of soda and pour in the warm soft dates and remaining water from the saucepan. Whisk on low for 5 minutes until everything has incorporated into a light brown, fairly thick cake batter. Once mixed, preheat the oven to 170°c. Line a large cake tray with parchment paper, about 6cm deep, 22cm wide and 38cm long; if you don't have a tray that big use two smaller ones and line with the parchment paper. Pour in the sticky toffee mix, place in the oven and bake for approximately 1 hour uncovered until golden and brown. The toffee pudding will double in size in the oven so after an hour stick a skewer into the thick part of the sponge and if it does not

come out clean, leave in the oven for a further 10 minutes. Once cooked remove and leave to completely cool. Once the sticky toffee has cooled, cut into portions, cling film individually and chill until needed. Freeze any leftover portions.

For the sticky toffee sauce place the butter and demerara sugar into a heavy based saucepan over a medium heat, let the butter melt and the sugar will start to dissolve into the butter (usually after about 5 minutes). Add the black treacle to the pan and bring the mixture up to a simmer, stirring with a wooden spoon constantly. Once simmering, pour in the double cream and bring back up to the boil. Once boiling, turn down the heat and simmer for 15 minutes; you will be left with a dark brown, glossy toffee sauce.

To Serve

Take the required amount of sticky toffee pudding pieces you need, remove cling film and warm through in a moderate oven for 10 minutes. Place a piece of the pudding on each plate and pour over the warm sauce. Serve either as it is or for a little more indulgence, add some vanilla ice cream or clotted cream.

PASSION FRUIT CRÈME BRÛLÉE WITH A SHORTBREAD BISCUIT

Ingredients | Serves 6

For the shortbread biscuits

125g plain flour

125g soft unsalted butter

50g caster sugar

1 organic egg yolk

1 orange, zest

1 lime, zest

1 vanilla pod, split and deseeded

1 tablespoon double cream

For the crème brûlée

4 passion fruit

125g caster sugar

6 medium egg yolks

600ml double cream

1 vanilla pod, split

To garnish

Caster sugar for glazing

Specialist equipment

Blow torch (or brown under a grill)

Crème brûlée is a great no-fuss dessert that can be made in advance, tastes delicious and is very simple to make.

Start the crème brûlée by putting the double cream, vanilla pod and seeds into a heavy based saucepan over a medium heat and slowly bringing it up to a simmer. Once the cream simmers, turn off the heat and leave the pan to one side. In a mixing bowl whisk the egg yolks and caster sugar together for 5 minutes until the mix appears paler, then slowly add the warm cream to the egg mix whisking constantly until the two mixes are combined together. It is important that you whisk quickly and that the cream you add is not too hot to avoid scrambling the eggs. Once combined, take the passion fruit, cut each one in half and scoop out the seeds dividing equally into six ramekins. Pour the crème brûlée mix into each ramekin and then transfer into a roasting tray. Pour water into the roasting tray so it comes half way up the side of the ramekins, we call this a bain-marie. Place the tray into a preheated oven at 140°c for 40 minutes until the custard has set. Once cooked remove the ramekins from the tray, allow to cool, then place them in the fridge and chill for at least 1 hour but preferably overnight.

For the shortbread biscuits preheat the oven to 160°c. In a large mixing bowl cream together the caster sugar and soft butter until you have a smooth crumbly texture. To that add the double cream, orange zest, lime zest, vanilla seeds and egg yolk and beat until fully incorporated. Sift the flour into this and mix together until a dough has formed. Line a large baking tray with a sheet of baking paper and lightly grease with butter. In your hands ball out each biscuit to about the size of table tennis ball, place them onto the baking paper leaving space between each biscuit. Once you have done this with all the dough, press down on each ball of the mix with your hands to flatten them to about ½cm thick. Place the tray in the oven and bake for 10 minutes until golden brown. Once out of the oven place the biscuits on a cake rack to cool.

To Serve

Remove the crème brûlée from the oven, dust with caster sugar and caramelise the sugar on top of the brûlée with a blow torch. If you do not have one place them under a grill for a few minutes. Place each brûlée on a plate and serve with the biscuits.

OLD FASHIONED
PLUM COBBLER

A cobbler is an old fashioned dessert which consists of stewed fruit with a scone topping that is then baked through in the oven. The top of the cobbler will be golden and crisp and underneath will be sweet and soft; try making it with any type of fruit you want.

Start by cutting the plumbs in half; remove the stone-seed from each one and then quarter. Place all the chopped plums into a heavy based saucepan and add the caster sugar, lemon juice, water and cornflour. Place over a high heat and bring to the boil, simmer for 5 minutes and mix everything together. Turn off the stove and leave to cool.

Before preparing the cobbler topping preheat the oven to 180°c. In a mixing bowl with a paddle attachment (or you could also use your hands) add the flour and cubed butter and mix until it resembles a fine crumb. Add the sugar, milk and egg to the flour mixture and beat together for a few minutes until you have a thick batter.

Take a large ovenproof serving dish or 6 individual ones and spoon in the plum mixture. With a tablespoon blob the batter all over the top of the fruit leaving little gaps between each spoonful. Place in the middle shelf of the oven and cook for 25 minutes until golden, the fruit will be bubbling in and around the crunchy scone topping.

To Serve

I like to serve it straight from the oven either on its own or with crème fraîche, vanilla ice cream or as it's a classic dessert, custard.

Ingredients | Serves 6

900g plums

100g caster sugar

1 lemon, juiced

200ml water

2 tablespoon cornflour

For the cobber topping

200g self-raising flour

75g butter, cubed

50g caster sugar

100ml whole milk

1 whole egg

CARAMELISED RICE PUDDING

The ultimate autumn dessert; warm, delicious, comforting, filling and one of the nation's most loved puddings.

This dessert could not be simpler. In a heavy based saucepan add the rice, double cream, nutmeg, caster sugar, vanilla pod and seeds. Place the pan over a medium heat and stir for 3 minutes. Add the milk to the pan and allow to gently simmer on the stove for 1 hour, stirring every 10 minutes until the rice pudding has softened and thickened. If too thick, just add a touch more milk to loosen. You will be left with a creamy, thick, delicious rice pudding. Before serving, have a taste and add any more sugar if you have a sweet tooth.

To Serve

Take the warm rice pudding and place into individual serving dishes. Sprinkle with the demerara sugar and glaze with a blow torch. If you do not have a blow torch place under a grill and caramelise. Serve immediately.

Ingredients | Serves 4-6

250g Arborio rice

450ml whole milk

300ml double cream

1 vanilla pod, split

Pinch of grated nutmeg

50g caster sugar

30g demerara sugar for caramelising

Specialist equipment

Blow torch (or brown under a grill)

WINTER

Winter is cold, the mood begins to change as the nights draw in but thankfully, this season has some fantastic things to offer us that should lift our spirits.

Beautiful root vegetables are everywhere; we have swede, turnip, celeriac, Jerusalem artichoke and parsnips.

The sea in winter is at its coldest and this produces some amazing seafood such as oysters, mussels and scallops. And don't forget the black truffle, my personal favourite; strong in flavour and the most beautiful taste.

This really is a comforting season, when we like to eat food that keeps us warm and makes us smile. So let's enjoy what this great country has to offer.

These dishes are simple to prepare, bold in flavour and will bring a smile to your diners.

CAULIFLOWER SOUP
WITH AN ONION BHAJI

Spices are very popular in British cuisine and I think the light spicing in my onion bhaji goes great with the creamy soup. It's a great alternative to just serving it with bread.

Ingredients | Serves 6-8
For the soup

2 large cauliflowers

1 large white onion

4 cloves garlic

50g butter

Olive oil

250ml double cream

Water or light chicken stock to cover (page 123)

Salt and pepper

For the onion bhaji

3 white onions

100g plain flour

Sea salt and black pepper

½ teaspoon turmeric

1 tablespoon mild curry powder

2 cloves garlic, finely chopped

1 whole egg

10g melted butter

1 bunch coriander, chopped

Approximately 100ml vegetable oil for frying

For the soup, peel and dice the onion and garlic, place into a heavy based saucepan with the butter and a drizzle of olive oil. Gently cook for a few minutes without colour. Meanwhile, remove the bottom of the cauliflower stalk and the outer leaves and discard. Cut off the florets and finely chop the inside stalk; it has great flavour so it should be used. Add the florets and stalk to the pan and cover with water or chicken stock, season with some sea salt and pepper and boil for 15 minutes or until the cauliflower is tender. Add the double cream then, with a ladle, carefully transfer to a blender and purée until smooth or place a stick blender in the pan and purée. Once smooth, return to the pan, adjust the seasoning and simmer on the stove until you have a beautifully thick and creamy soup.

I am no expert at making onion bhajis and there are many different ways to make them but this is a recipe that I think works and tastes great. The light spicing goes really well with the creamy soup. Peel and finely slice the white onions and add them to a bowl, then to this add the plain flour, turmeric, curry powder, chopped garlic, coriander, egg, melted butter, sea salt

and black pepper. Mix everything together with your hands and you will be left with a slightly wet sticky bhaji mix. In a shallow frying pan, cover the bottom of the pan 1cm thick in vegetable oil over a medium heat. Take little handfuls of the bhaji mix out of the bowl and mould them into patties in your hand, carefully place them in the oil one by one and gently fry for 3 minutes until golden. Turn them over and fry for a further 3 minutes until the other side is also golden. A gentle fry is fine – you do not need the temperature of the stove too high, so if they begin to fry too quickly, turn down the heat. Once cooked, carefully remove the bhajis and place on kitchen cloth to remove any excess oil. Do this a few bhajis at a time until all the mix is used.

To Serve

If you have made the onion bhajis in advance, warm them gently under a grill on a tray. Spoon the soup into your serving bowls and place the bhajis in the centre of the table, drizzle some good quality olive oil over the soup and serve.

This is a great starter, the gamey flavour of the pigeon matched with the sweetness of the shallots in the tatin is a match made in heaven.

PAN FRIED BREAST OF WOOD PIGEON, SHALLOT AND THYME TATIN AND A PIGEON SAUCE

Ingredients | Serves 6

3 wood pigeon, breasts removed, bones saved

For the tatin

8 banana shallots

½ bunch thyme

500g block of puff pastry

1 egg, beaten

50g butter

Olive oil

Flour, for dusting

Sea salt and pepper

For the pigeon sauce

Pigeon carcasses

1 juniper berry

1 bay leaf

1 sprig thyme

5 peppercorns

1 celery stick

1 small onion

1 carrot

1 bulb garlic

300ml red wine

100ml tomato juice

Ask your butcher for three whole pigeons and get them to remove the breasts and save the carcasses for stock. Keep the breasts in the fridge until needed. In a heavy based saucepan colour the pigeon carcasses with a drizzle of olive oil, add the juniper berry, sprig of thyme, bay leaf, peppercorns, stick of chopped celery, onion, carrot and bulb of garlic split in half. Cook in the pan for a few minutes mixing everything around, then cover with water, about 2 litres. Simmer the stock for 2 hours skimming any fat that rises to the top. Strain the stock through a fine sieve into another pan, add the red wine and tomato juice, return to the stove and boil to reduce by three-quarters, this will take about an hour. When you have a nice thick sauce that coats the back of a spoon turn off the heat and the sauce is ready.

Preheat the oven to 180°c ready for the shallot tatin. On a large metal baking tray add a sheet of baking paper. Drizzle over some olive oil and rub it all over the baking paper. Take the thyme and remove the leaves by running your fingers down the stalks. Sprinkle the thyme over the tray then season with sea salt and black pepper. Peel the shallots and slice them in half lengthways. Place the flat side of the shallots onto the tray in rows about four along until the tray is full with shallot. Take the butter and disperse it evenly in little bits over the shallots; this will melt through and help caramelise when cooking. The next step is to roll out the pastry on a cold surface dusted with flour, roll it a few millimetres thick then place the sheet of pastry over the shallots. Cut off any excess pastry then brush the beaten egg over the top of the pastry. Place the tray into the oven and cook for 25 minutes or until the pastry is golden brown. When it is cooked remove the tray and leave to cool. Then carefully flip the tatin over onto a clean surface, remove the tray and baking paper and you'll be left with a beautiful golden shallot and thyme tatin. Slice it into 6 squares or cut it out with a metal cutter, discard the excess and place the portion onto a clean tray ready for later.

To Serve

Take the pigeon breasts out of the fridge, pull off and discard the skin then season the breasts with sea salt and black pepper. Heat a frying pan on the stove with a drizzle of olive oil. Once hot add the pigeon breasts on the side the skin was, pan fry for 2 minutes then turn over the breasts. Add the butter and spoon over the hot foaming butter. Do this for a further 2 minutes, this will colour and keep the pigeon breasts lovely and moist. After 2 more minutes of basting transfer the pigeon to a tray and pour over the butter and leave to rest for 5 minutes. Gently heat the tatin under a grill. Place a piece of tatin on each plate, half the pigeon breasts lengthways and place a breast on each plate, drizzle around some sauce and serve. The pigeon should be medium rare, juicy and tender.

POACHED DUCK EGG WITH CAULIFLOWER, CRISPY SHALLOT, PARMA HAM AND PEA SHOOTS

I love the different textures in this light starter. The soft poached egg provides a great sauce over the sweet cauliflower and creamy purée, plus there's the crunch from the shallots which is all finished off with the saltiness from the soft Parma ham and fresh pea shoots. It's delicious.

Ingredients | Serves 6

6 duck eggs

50ml white wine vinegar

For the cauliflower

2 cauliflowers

1 bunch chives, chopped

50g butter

Salt and pepper

For the cauliflower purée

The left over cauliflower hearts

100ml double cream

100g melted butter

For the crispy shallot

2 banana shallots

50g cornflour

Vegetable oil for shallow frying

To garnish

1 punnet pea shoots

150g Parma ham

For any vegetarians out there this starter works just as well without the Parma ham and the duck eggs can easily be substituted for hen eggs if that is your preference.

The cooking of the duck egg can be done in various ways. For anyone with a water bath, a more professional piece of equipment, place the duck eggs into the bath for 2 hours at 62°c, then remove the eggs, crack the shell and carefully remove the egg. A second way is to steam the eggs at 62°c for 1½ hours, then crack the shell and remove the egg, and lastly, there is the conventional way. Bring a pan of water to the boil with the white wine vinegar. Just before cooking take a whisk and create a whirlpool in the water, crack the shell and tip the egg into the middle of the pan, simmer for 3 minutes then carefully remove the egg with a slotted spoon, trim off any excess white, sprinkle over some sea salt and serve.

The egg sits on a bed of cauliflower. Take the cauliflowers and using a sharp knife, chop around the outside so that you are shaving the sides off all the florets until you are left with a smooth round cauliflower. We want all the pieces that fall off, chop them so they are fine and keep in a container. Save the heart of the cauliflower for the purée. Just before serving place the cauliflower pieces into a saucepan with a drizzle of olive oil, the butter and chopped chives, gently heat on the stove so the cauliflower is warm but still retains its crunch. Once hot season with sea salt and pepper.

Cut the left over heart of cauliflower into a rough dice, cover with water and cook on the stove until soft. Strain through a colander and put the soft cauliflower into a food processor; liquidise with the double cream and butter until you have a smooth purée. If the purée is too thick, add a touch more cream to loosen it. Season with sea salt and pepper then serve.

Peel the shallots then thinly slice into rings, separate each ring and dust with cornflour, sea salt and pepper. Cover the bottom of a large frying pan with vegetable oil over a medium heat. Shake off any excess flour and place the shallot rings into the pan, fry until golden moving them around with a spoon so they get a nice even colour. When crisp, remove from the pan with a slotted spoon and drain the shallots on some kitchen paper. Season with sea salt and leave in a cool dry place. You will be left with really crispy shallot rings.

To Serve

Spoon the purée into the centre of each plate, top with a pile of the cauliflower pieces then top with a poached egg. Lay around a few slices of Parma ham then garnish with the crispy shallots and pea shoots.

HAND DIVED SCALLOP, JERUSALEM ARTICHOKE PURÉE AND WINTER TRUFFLE

Hand dived scallops are much larger, juicier, sweeter and gentler on the seabed than the dredged varieties. Dredging damages the seabed whereas hand diving supports a more sustainable and environmentally friendly fishing method. Yes, they are more expensive, but they're worth every penny and are readily available from your local fishmongers.

Ingredients | Serves 6

6 hand dived scallops, out of shell, roe removed

1 lemon, juiced

Olive oil

For the artichoke purée

200g Jerusalem artichokes, peeled

125ml double cream

25g butter

Sea salt

To garnish

55-85g winter truffle

This dish is true luxury; the smooth purée with the sweet scallop and lashings of truffle is amazing. I do however completely understand the expense of this dish, so I have found an alternative. Fresh truffles are hugely expensive but there are now preserved truffles readily available online, the flavour is not as strong but it is a more budget-friendly way to add the appearance of truffle and some subtle flavour to the dish.

Peel, dice and then wash the Jerusalem artichokes under a cold tap. Transfer to a heavy based saucepan and cover with water. Place on the stove and bring up to a boil – once boiling simmer until the artichokes are soft – this will take about 45 minutes. Strain through a sieve to remove the water, add the double cream and butter to the dry pan and place back on the stove. Add the soft artichokes to the cream and butter and simmer everything together for 2 minutes. Purée in a blender until you have a silky smooth purée, season with sea salt and set aside.

Remove the white mussel from each scallop and discard the roe and skirt (Please speak to your fishmonger if you haven't done this before), save and clean the shells for serving if you choose. The roe can be frozen and used in fish sauces and even dried and powdered as a seasoning but for this dish we do not require them. Place a large frying pan onto a high heat, season the scallop with a little sea salt, drizzle with olive oil and gently place into the pan. Pan fry for 2 minutes but don't shake the pan, leave to caramelise slightly, add a knob of butter then turn each scallop over and cook for a further minute. Squeeze over some fresh lemon juice then remove from the pan and place onto some kitchen towel.

To Serve

Either serve on a plate or in the shells that the scallops came from. Place a scallop on each serving dish, add a dot of the purée and serve straight away. I like to grate my truffle on a fine grater at the table over each scallop just before eating to add theatre and also keep that intense flavour on the dish.

Poaching the guinea fowl breast like this keeps them juicy, moist, full of flavour and it's also very healthy for you.

POACHED GUINEA FOWL BREAST, PARSNIP PURÉE, GRILLED BABY LEEK AND A MADEIRA SAUCE

Ingredients | Serves 6

6 guinea fowl breasts
1 leek
1 carrot
2 celery sticks
1 white onion
5 peppercorns
1 bay leaf
1 bulb garlic, split
1 sprig thyme
2 litres water
Salt and pepper

For the sauce

2 litres white chicken stock (see page 123)
200ml Madeira
200ml red wine
75ml tomato juice
1 bulb garlic, split

For the parsnip purée

4 parsnips
200ml double cream
50g butter

To garnish

18 baby leeks
Extra virgin olive oil

For the sauce, place the chicken stock, split bulb of garlic, Madeira, red wine and tomato juice into a heavy based saucepan. Put onto the stove and reduce by three-quarters or until you have a thick sauce that coats the back of a spoon. Once reduced, season with salt and pepper and strain through a fine sieve into a smaller pan ready to heat when you need it.

To cook the guinea fowl, start by roughly dicing the leek, carrot, celery and onion, give them a quick wash under some cold water then place into a heavy based saucepan with a bulb of garlic spilt in half, the bay leaf, peppercorns and the sprig of thyme. Add the water and place on the stove top and bring to the boil. As soon as it starts boiling add the guinea fowl breasts, making sure they are covered with water (you may need to add more). Bring the pan back to the boil then reduce the heat and simmer for 12 minutes. Once simmered, turn off the heat and leave in the hot stock for a further 12 minutes.

Peel and dice the parsnips, place into a saucepan, cover with water and simmer until tender. Once tender, heat the cream and butter in a separate pan. Strain the parsnip through a colander to remove the water. Place the parsnip, hot cream and butter into a blender and purée until smooth. Season with sea salt and pepper.

I like to leave my baby leeks whole. Bring a pan of water with a pinch of salt to the boil, add the leeks and cook for 1 minute then remove the leeks and cool in ice water. Once cool simply rub them with olive oil, season with sea salt and black pepper then either grill for 2 minutes each side over a medium heat on a chargrill or, if you do not have a chargrill, just place under a grill for 2 minutes on each side.

To Serve

Place a spoon of purée on each plate and sit the guinea fowl breast on top. Add the grilled leeks and spoon over the sauce. You can also serve with bowls of creamy mashed potato.

SLOW COOKED PORK BELLY, TURNIP PURÉE, ROAST PLUM AND TURNIP TOPS

For me, pork belly and plum is a match made in heaven; the sharpness of the plum cuts through the fattiness of the pork belly perfectly.

Ingredients | Serves 4-6	For the turnip purée	To garnish
For the pork belly		
2kg pork belly, skin removed	5 turnips	6 plums
4 star anise	200ml whole milk	1 sprig thyme
5g sea salt	100ml double cream	The green turnip tops
5g peppercorns	5g butter	red wine sauce (page 124)
5g coriander seeds	Salt and pepper	
1 bay leaf		

Ask your butcher to remove the skin and bones from the pork belly and keep the skin for crackling. With a pestle and mortar grind the sea salt, peppercorns, bay leaf, star anise and coriander seeds then season the top of the pork belly with the rub. Once you have seasoned the meat take some tin foil and wrap the belly. Preheat the oven to 150°c, place the tin foiled belly into a roasting tray then put in the oven for 4 hours. Once cooked, turn the oven off and leave to cool. Remove the tray and tip any juices into a separate container and save for later. Discard the tin foil then wrap the belly in cling film, place it onto a baking tray then place another baking tray on top and put into the fridge. Put something heavy on top of the pork belly like a large milk carton and set in the fridge for 24 hours, or at least a minimum of 12 hours. The reason for doing this is so we flatten out the belly and it will set with an even thickness so when we roast it the next day it will cook evenly, also it helps with the presentation.

For the skin, preheat the oven to 180°c, take a pair of scissors and cut into ½cm strips. Place the strips onto a baking tray lined with greaseproof paper and season with sea salt. Cook in the oven for 20 minutes, once cooked put the crackling on a cake rack and leave to dry overnight.

Buy the turnips from a local greengrocer and get them with the turnip tops still attached. Remove the turnip tops and wash them under a cold tap. Place onto a cloth and chill until needed. Peel and dice the turnips then place into a heavy based saucepan and add

the milk, cream, seasoning and simmer until the turnip is soft. Place into a blender and purée until smooth. If it's too thick, add a little melted butter and purée again to loosen, check the seasoning and adjust if needed.

Take a sharp knife and run it through the middle of each plum, when you hit the stone run the knife around the outside then pull the plums carefully in half, remove the stones and discard. Drizzle some olive oil over a roasting tray, then with some paper towels rub the oil evenly over the tray. Pick some thyme leaves and sprinkle onto the tray, then season the tray with some sea salt and pepper. Place each plum half into the tray flesh side down. Place the tray into a preheated oven at 180°c and roast for 10 minutes until they start to soften.

To Serve

Remove the pork belly from the fridge, unwrap and slice into four to six portions. In a frying pan, heat a tablespoon of olive oil over a medium heat, place the belly pieces skin side down and brown for a few minutes. Once brown transfer to a tray and heat through in a preheated oven at 180°c for 10 minutes. Heat a knob of butter in a pan and gently warm through the turnip tops; they just need warming not cooking as they are so tender. Season with sea salt and pepper. Spoon the purée onto each plate, add a few pieces of roasted plum, the wilted turnip tops and a piece of pork belly. Drizzle over some red wine sauce or the cooking juices and serve.

BEEF FILLET, BURNT ONION AND ROAST PARSNIP WITH A RED WINE AND THYME SAUCE

A tender melt in the mouth fillet steak, sweet honey roasted parsnips and burnt onion all finished off with some peppery watercress and a rich sauce… it's a great winter warmer.

Ingredients | Serves 6
6 good quality British beef fillet steaks (225-255g each)
For the burnt onion
6 banana shallots or small white onions
150g butter
olive oil
100ml white wine or chicken stock (page 123)

For the roast parsnips
6 parsnips
2 tablespoons clear honey
For the sauce
Red wine gravy (page 124)
½ bunch thyme
To garnish
1 bunch watercress

Fillet steak is my steak of preference for this dish but by all means use any steak that you wish; rump, t-bone or ribeye are also great options. I always find speaking to my local butcher and asking what good quality cuts of steak are the best way to do it, they will point you in the right direction.

Take your steaks out of the fridge one hour before cooking to bring them to room temperature, pat them dry with a cloth to remove any moisture. When you want to cook your steak's place a frying pan on the stove over a high heat. Season the meat with sea salt, not pepper as it will burn, and then rub with olive oil. Once the pan is smoking hot carefully place the steak's in the pan. Sear the meat on both sides, flipping the steak over every minute to caramelise the outside of the meat. We caramelise the meat quickly to create flavour and to lock in all the steak's juices. Cook the steak like this for about 4 minutes and it will give you a nice medium rare steak. However, if you want the steak cooked more or less, the easiest way to make sure your meat is cooked perfectly, is to use a digital probe. Place the probe into the middle off the thickest part of the meat. For rare, the core temperature needs to be 50°c, medium-rare 55°c, medium 60°c and well done 70°c. For anything over medium rare, finish in an oven preheated at 180°c. Once your steak is cooked to your liking place it on a clean tray and allow to rest for 5 minutes to relax the meat. Slice and season the exposed flesh with sea salt and pepper.

The burnt onion is a more 'on trend' way of cooking that I think you'll be interested in. It adds a slight bitterness and complements the meat very well. Take the shallots or small white onions and cut them in half lengthways through the root leaving the skin on, this will protect and let the onion almost steam within its own skin. Add a drizzle of olive oil to a large frying pan over a medium heat. As the oil begins to smoke add the onions flesh side down and begin to caramelise, turn one over with a spoon after a few minutes and check to see it is caramelising. Once the

flesh side of the onion has burnt add the butter and with a spoon keep basting the butter over the onion for 2 minutes, this will add flavour and keep the onions moist. Flip the onions over so the flesh is now facing towards you then add the wine or stock and place a lid over the pan and steam for 4 minutes. Remove the onions onto a tray and pour over the juices and leave them to cool slightly. Once manageable with your hands, take off the skin and separate the little onion cups. Season the onion flesh with some sea salt and pepper, and before serving just heat them through a pan with a touch of butter.

To roast the parsnips preheat an oven to 180°c. Cut the top and bottom off each parsnip, peel, quarter and remove some of the root. Bring a pan of water to the boil and add the parsnips, cook for 2 minutes then drain, this will soften them slightly and makes them extra crispy. Once the water has drained give them a shake and season them with sea salt, pepper, the honey and a drizzle of olive oil. Mix well, tip onto a roasting tray and roast for 20 minutes or until soft and crisp, turning them every 5 minutes to glaze evenly.

Remove the thyme leaves from the stalks and add to the red wine gravy. Heat gently on the stove.

Chef's Tip

For a quick and easy sauce when you remove the steaks from the frying pan, add 150ml of red wine and the thyme leaves to the pan. Scrape the bits off the bottom and reduce. Once reduced by half remove the pan from the heat and whisk in 100g of cold butter to create a glossy sauce.

To Serve

Create a salad by mixing the parsnip, onion shells and watercress together. Divide evenly between the plates and add the sliced steak. Drizzle over some sauce and serve.

OVEN-ROASTED CORNISH COD, CAULIFLOWER AND PEARL BARLEY COUSCOUS, ROASTED COBNUTS, HOME DRIED RAISINS AND A SAUTERNES SAUCE

This is a dish with great textures and flavours; the cauliflower is shaved into couscous and the homemade raisins go perfectly with the fish, which is all finished off with the sweet Sauternes sauce. It's a very balanced and beautiful dish.

Ingredients | Serves 6

800g cod fillet, skin removed

100g sea salt

Olive oil

50g butter

For the couscous

250g pearl barley

1 large cauliflower

50g butter

½ bunch dill, chopped

1 lemon, juiced

For the Sauternes sauce

500ml fish stock (page 122)

150ml double cream

375ml dessert wine

1 lemon, juiced

Pinch cayenne pepper

1 shallot

To garnish

100g toasted cobnuts

1 bunch seedless green grapes

To make the raisins take all the grapes off the stalks, place them onto a metal tray and pop them into an oven preheated at 40°c. Leave them in the oven for 10 hours; I generally put them in overnight. After 10 hours they will have dried out and shrivelled into raisins but will still be slightly juicy inside. Tip them into an airtight container and store in a cool dry place until needed.

The couscous is a play on words; the way the cauliflower is cut resembles couscous. Start by soaking the pearl barley for 1 hour in cold water then tip the water away. Place the soaked barley into a saucepan, cover with water and simmer for 15 minutes or until tender. Once cooked, strain and cool down with cold water. Take the cauliflower and using a sharp knife chop around the outside so that you are shaving the sides off all the florets until you are left with a smooth round cauliflower. All the pieces that fall off look like couscous, chop them so they are fine and keep in a container. When you want to serve the couscous place the butter and some olive oil in a pan over a medium heat, add the pearl barley and cauliflower and heat through, the cauliflower needs no cooking as it is so fine. Warm through then season with salt and pepper, squeeze in the lemon juice and add the chopped dill. Stir and it's ready to serve.

For the Sauternes sauce, peel and chop the shallot, add it to a heavy based saucepan with the dessert wine and reduce by half, then add the fish stock and reduce by half again. Add a pinch of cayenne, lemon juice and double cream, season with sea salt and pepper and reduce by three-quarters until you are left with a thick creamy sauce. Strain through a fine sieve into a smaller pan, adjust the seasoning and heat back up when needed.

Break the cobnuts with the back of a pan, if you do not have these hazelnuts work just fine. Place them onto a metal tray and colour slightly under a grill.

Just before cooking the fish preheat the oven to 200°c. Lay the fish fillet in a dish and sprinkle the salt over the fish and place in the fridge for 1 hour. After 1 hour, wash the salt off and dry, cut into six portions and cling film each one tightly. Place in the fridge to firm up for a minimum of 1 hour. To cook the fish place a non-stick ovenproof pan over a medium heat. When the pan is hot add a touch of oil and place the fillets in the pan on the side the skin was, season with sea salt and pepper then fry for 2 minutes until golden. Add the butter then flip over the fish, place the pan in the oven and cook for a further 4-5 minutes. Remove the pan and leave the fish to rest for 5 minutes.

To Serve

Place a pile of the pearl barley and cauliflower couscous onto each plate, top with a piece of fish and scatter the raisins and cobnuts around the plate. Drizzle around the sauce, scatter over a few herbs and serve.

DARK CHOCOLATE AND HAZELNUT FONDANT, MUESLI, CHOCOLATE SOIL AND FROZEN YOGHURT

Ingredients | Serves 6-8

For the frozen yoghurt

300ml water

80g caster sugar

300g sheep's yoghurt

300g cow's yoghurt

1 lemon, juiced

For the chocolate fondant

175g dark chocolate

40g dark chocolate to put in the centre

165g unsalted butter

5 eggs yolks

165g caster sugar

200g plain flour

100g finely chopped hazelnuts

50g soft unsalted butter to line moulds

For the soil

75g dark chocolate

25g milk chocolate

60g melted unsalted butter

80g cocoa powder

120g caster sugar

50g plain flour

To garnish

100g muesli

Everyone likes a chocolate fondant and when made correctly they are the ultimate dessert. It is essential to cook them for the correct amount time to ensure that runny chocolate centre, add that with the crunch of the muesli and the cool frozen yoghurt and I guarantee this is a pudding that will leave you with a smile.

The frozen yoghurt can be made days in advance so it's always good to make this before then it's another job ticked off the list early, making your life much easier. Start by putting both types of yoghurt, water, lemon juice and sugar in a bowl and whisk for a few minutes to incorporate all the ingredients together. Once mixed pour the yoghurt mix into a sealed plastic container and freeze. Leave for 24 hours. The next day remove from the freezer and with a fork begin to scrape the yoghurt into another plastic container, this will give you a snow like texture, it might take a while but once you have scraped it into snow, re-freeze in another container until needed.

To make the chocolate fondants preheat the oven to 180°c. Start by lining six to eight dariole moulds with melted butter using a pastry brush then sprinkle the finely chopped hazelnuts into each mould. Roll the mould around ensuring each one has an even coat of chopped hazelnut around the inside; the hazelnuts will stick to the melted butter, then tip out any excess nuts from each mould, place on a tray and store in the fridge until needed. Melt the chocolate and butter in a bowl over a pan of simmering water. In a separate bowl whisk the egg yolks and caster sugar together until creamy and light. Once the chocolate and butter has melted pour it into the eggs and sugar and whisk together until fully incorporated. Once mixed, sift in the flour and mix together with a wooden spoon or paddle in a mixing bowl and beat together to form a smooth batter. Remove the moulds from the fridge and fill each one three-quarters of the way up, place a little piece of chocolate in the centre of each one. Place back in the fridge until needed.

The chocolate soil is a little added garnish, it will keep in your store cupboard for a month in an airtight container so you can make this in advance. Also it's a great little garnish to sprinkle onto the plate to hold ice cream or even to sprinkle over a bowl of vanilla ice cream. Start by melting the chocolates together in a bowl over simmering water. Once melted add the remaining ingredients and mix together with a wooden spoon. Pour out on a tray lined with greaseproof paper and chill for two hours in the fridge. Place in a preheated oven at 170°c and cook for 15 minutes, remove then leave to cool. Once cool, scrape the chocolate with a fork into a container and it will crumble into a soil like texture, place in a tupperware container and store in a dry place.

To Serve

Preheat the oven to 180°c. Place the muesli onto a tray and gently toast under a grill, then leave to one side to cool. Remove the chocolate fondants from the fridge and place in the centre of the oven, cooking for 11 minutes. I always like to cook one in advance just to check the cooking time is correct as each oven does tend to be slightly different. After 11 minutes the top will be crisp but when you touch it the fondant will still feel soft and we want that gooey centre. Whilst the fondants cook, garnish each plate with a pile of the frozen yoghurt, then sprinkle the toasted muesli and chocolate soil around each plate. Remove the fondants once cooked then carefully tip each one out onto a clean cloth in your hand then transfer to each plate. Serve straight away and when you cut into it the chocolate will ooze out of the middle.

Even if you're not a peanut butter lover I can assure you this dessert will change your mind. The delicious light mousse with the crunch of the hazelnuts and sweetness from the glazed banana makes for one of my ultimate all time favourite desserts and it just happens to be my biggest seller.

PEANUT BUTTER MOUSSE, TOASTED HAZELNUTS AND GLAZED BANANA

Ingredients | Serves 6-8
For the peanut butter mousse
334g whole eggs
180g sifted icing sugar
480g double cream
5 gelatine leaves
440g smooth peanut butter
5 egg whites
To garnish
4 bananas
100g blanched hazelnuts, toasted
Icing sugar for dusting
Specialist equipment
Blow torch (or brown under a grill)

The peanut butter mousse needs a minimum of 3 hours to set in the fridge so I always make this the day before so that when it comes to plating the dessert, all we have to do is glaze the bananas.

There is quite a lot of pan juggling with this dessert to get all the elements together at the end so it's essential to be prepared and organised. I have broken the dessert down into three stages.

First we need to soften the gelatine; do this by placing the gelatine leaves in a container and cover with cold water, for approximately 5 minutes.

Stage 1

In a large bowl add the sifted icing sugar and the cracked, weighed whole eggs, place a heavy based saucepan on the stove, fill half way with water and leave it on the stove on the lowest setting so it barely simmers. Place the bowl onto the pan, making sure the water does not touch the bottom of the bowl and whisk the eggs and sugar together; this will cook the eggs. It is important to make sure the temperature is not too high and also that you whisk constantly so that the eggs do not scramble. If the water was to boil the bowl would get too hot, leaving us with scrambled egg, so it's very important to have the stove on its lowest setting. Whisk for 15 minutes, the egg and sugar mixture will double in size and become much paler and very smooth, in turn cooking the eggs very gently, this is called a sabayon. Once the eggs are cooked, remove the bowl from the pan and leave to one side.

Stage 2

In a separate pan gently heat the double cream. As soon as it starts to simmer, remove from the heat, take the soft gelatine leaves out of the water and whisk into the double cream until they have dissolved, then pour the warm cream over the peanut butter and mix with a wooden spoon until you are left with a smooth, fully incorporated peanut butter paste.

Stage 3

In a bowl, whisk the egg whites until you have soft peaks.

Now we have completed our three stages, we need to incorporate everything together. Pour the peanut butter (stage 2) into the sabayon (stage 1) and whisk until fully incorporated and smooth. Once mixed, take the whipped egg whites (stage 3) and gently fold into the peanut butter mix as gently as possible as to not knock out any air bubbles. We want it as light as possible. Once mixed, pour into a container and set in the fridge for a minimum of 3 hours.

To Serve

Gently toast the hazelnuts under the grill. Peel the bananas, chop in half lengthways, dust with icing sugar on a metal tray and glaze with a blow torch. If you don't have a blow torch, place under a grill until golden. Place two pieces of banana on each plate, spoon on the peanut butter mousse and scatter over the toasted hazelnuts. This dessert is by far one of my biggest sellers; everyone that tries it falls in love instantly. I like to serve mine with a toffee sauce.

BROWN SUGAR CAKE WITH A BUTTERSCOTCH SAUCE

You can't beat the smell of this cake fresh out of the oven, topped with an indulgent butterscotch sauce that will leave you coming back for more.

Ingredients | Serves 6-8

For the brown sugar cake

100g caster sugar

220g demerara sugar

750g melted unsalted butter

8 whole eggs

500g self-raising flour

For the butterscotch sauce

250g unsalted butter

225g demerara sugar

4 tablespoons of golden syrup

600ml double cream

Preheat an oven to 160°c. Start by placing the caster sugar, demerara sugar and eggs in a bowl with a paddle attachment, mix on full for 5 minutes until fully mixed. Turn down the mixer and slowly add the melted butter, then add the flour and mix for a few minutes until fully incorporated and you are left with a thick cake batter. Pour the mix into a lined cake tin or six to eight mini cake tins. This can also be made the old fashioned way with a wooden spoon and bowl if you don't have a mixer, the recipe still works every time. If you are cooking one big cake place on the middle shelf and bake for 1 hour 20 minutes, for smaller individual tins bake for 50 minutes.

For the butterscotch sauce place the butter and demerara sugar into a heavy based saucepan over a medium heat, let the butter melt and the sugar will start to dissolve into the butter after about 5 minutes. Add the golden syrup to the pan and bring the mixture up to a simmer stirring with a wooden spoon constantly. Once simmering, pour in the double cream and bring back up to the boil. Once boiling, turn down the heat and simmer for 15 minutes; you will be left with a thick, glossy butterscotch sauce.

To Serve

I like to serve this straight from the oven to get the best out of this cake, slice or leave whole if small, pour over the sauce and serve straight away. If there is any left over, it's a great afternoon snack with a cup of tea or coffee.

POACHED BABY PEAR, COCONUT PUDDING AND HAZELNUT PRALINE

This dessert is refreshing, light and a great way to finish off a meal. The juicy poached pears with the creamy coconut and the crunch from the praline is a match made in heaven.

Ingredients | Serves 4-6	For the coconut pudding	For the praline
For the poached pears	500g coconut cream	70g caster sugar
6 small ripe English pears	50g caster sugar	100g hazelnuts
Water to cover	100g water	
225g caster sugar	2g agar agar	
1 vanilla pod, split	½ gelatine leaf	
1 lemon		

This is another dessert that can be made a day in advance meaning on the day your friends are over you spend less time in the kitchen and more time socialising.

For the poached pears, put the water and sugar into a heavy based saucepan and bring up to the boil. Once boiling, reduce the heat and simmer. Split the vanilla pod in half, scrape out the seeds and add to the water. Halve the lemon and squeeze into the water. Peel all the pears, keeping them whole and add to the pan ensuring they are covered. Simmer for 5 minutes or a little longer if your pears are large or not as ripe. Turn off the heat and leave the pears in the stock syrup until cool. Once cool, transfer the pears and liquid to a container and chill until needed.

Coconut cream can be found in most supermarkets. To make the coconut pudding, place the caster sugar, water, agar agar and gelatine in a saucepan and bring to the boil. Once boiling, simmer for 2 minutes then whisk in the coconut cream and simmer for a further 2 minutes. Pour the mixture into a tray and set in the fridge overnight. The next day take the set coconut cream out of the fridge, place into a blender and blend into a smooth purée, then spoon it into a squeezy bottle and leave in the fridge until needed.

The praline is very simple to make but needs your constant attention otherwise it can burn very quickly. Place the caster sugar into a dry, small pan, place over a low heat on the stove. Now the trick here is not to stir or touch the sugar and also not to have the heat too high. The sugar will gradually dissolve, as it dissolves give the pan a little shake and let the sugar melt into a golden brown caramel, keeping the temperature low to avoid burning. As soon as the sugar has melted (this will take about 10 minutes), add the whole, peeled hazelnuts, mix with a spoon and tip straight out onto a tray lined with greaseproof paper. Be very careful not to touch the caramel as it reaches very high temperatures. Leave the praline for at least 30 minutes to cool. Once cool place the praline into a blender and blitz into a rough crumb and store in a dry place until needed.

To Serve

Remove the pears from the poaching liquid. Cut each pear into quarters and cut out the stalk. Place 4 pieces of pear on each plate, squeeze dots of the coconut pudding around the plate and sprinkle over the crunchy, nutty praline. This has great textures and is one of my favourite desserts.

THE BASICS

STOCKS AND SAUCES
FISH STOCK

Makes about 500ml

1kg fish bones, washed and chopped

1 white onion, peeled and chopped

1 star anise

5 peppercorns

1 fennel bulb, chopped

1 celery stick, chopped

½ teaspoon fennel seeds

10 parsley stalks

Place all the ingredients into a large saucepan and cover with water. Bring up to the boil then once it starts, reduce the heat to a minimum. Skim any impurities off the top with a ladle. Simmer the stock for 25 minutes skimming any other impurities that may rise to the top. After 25 minutes strain the stock into a container through a fine sieve and leave to cool. Once cool place a lid on the container and store in the fridge for 3 days or up to 3 months in a freezer.

FISH SAUCE

Makes about 300ml

500ml fish stock

1 shallot, peeled and chopped

100ml white wine

½ lemon, juiced

50ml double cream

Salt and pepper

Place the white wine and shallot into a heavy based saucepan on a high heat, reduce by half and add the fish stock. Reduce by half again and then add the double cream. Reduce until you have a sauce consistency that coats the back of a spoon, strain through a fine sieve and season with lemon juice, sea salt and pepper. This will keep in the fridge for up to 3 days.

GAME STOCK

Makes about 1½ litres

2kg game bones (pigeon, pheasant, partridge, etc.)

1 pigs' trotter, split in half

1 white onion, roughly peeled and chopped

2 celery sticks, roughly chopped

2 carrots, roughly chopped

1 bay leaf

5 juniper berries

1 bulb garlic, split in half

Preheat your oven to 200°c. Place the bones and pigs' trotter into a large roasting tray and roast for 30 minutes in the oven. Once roasted remove the bones with a pair of tongs and place them into a large saucepan. Add all the remaining ingredients and cover with cold water. Bring to the boil and then reduce the heat to a minimum. Skim any impurities off the stock with a ladle and leave to gently simmer for 6 hours, skimming any other impurities off with a ladle every hour. After 6 hours strain the stock into a container and leave to cool. Once cool store the stock in a fridge for up to 3 days or in a freezer for up to 2 months.

GAME SAUCE

Makes about 600ml

1½ litres game stock

1 bulb garlic, spilt in half

1 shallot, peeled and roughly chopped

½ bottle red wine

100ml tomato juice

Salt and pepper

In a heavy based saucepan add the shallot, garlic and red wine and put the pan onto a high heat. Reduce by half then add the game stock and tomato juice. Reduce by about three quarters or until you have a sauce consistency that coats the back of a spoon. Strain the sauce through a fine sieve into a container and season with sea salt and black pepper. Once cool, the sauce can be stored in the fridge for up to 5 days.

WHITE CHICKEN STOCK

Makes about 2 litres

2kg chicken wings

1 white onion, peeled and chopped

1 bay leaf

5 peppercorns

2 celery sticks, roughly chopped

2 carrots, roughly chopped

1 bulb garlic, chopped in half

Place all of the ingredients into a large saucepan. Cover with cold water and bring to the boil. Once boiling, reduce the heat to a minimum and skim any impurities off the top of the liquid with a ladle. Leave the stock to gently simmer for 6 hours, skimming it every hour with a ladle to remove any more impurities. After 6 hours, strain the stock through a fine sieve and leave to cool. Once cool the stock can be stored in a fridge for 3 days, or up to 2 months in a freezer.

CHICKEN SAUCE

Makes about 500ml

2 litres white chicken stock

1 bulb garlic, split in half

1 shallot, peeled and chopped

½ bottle white wine

50ml double cream

Salt and pepper

In a heavy based saucepan, add the white wine, garlic and shallot and turn the heat to high. Reduce by half and add the chicken stock, then reduce by three quarters and add the double cream. Reduce on high until you have a thick sauce that coats the back of a spoon, strain through a fine sieve and season with sea salt and pepper. This sauce can be stored in a fridge for up to 3 days.

MEAT STOCK

Makes about 1½ litres

1½kg beef or veal bones, chopped

1kg chicken bones

1 pigs' trotter, split

2 carrots, washed and roughly chopped

4 celery sticks, washed and roughly chopped

1 large white onion, peeled and roughly chopped

½ bunch thyme

1 bulb garlic, split in half

Preheat an oven to 200°c. Place the bones and pig's trotter into a large roasting tray and roast for 45 minutes, or until golden brown. Transfer the bones to a large saucepan and add the rest of the ingredients. Place the saucepan on the stove top and cover with cold water, put the gas on full to bring the stock up to temperature, but do not boil. Once the stock begins to gently simmer reduce the heat to the minimum setting, take a ladle and skim any fat off the top of the liquid. Leave the stock for 6 hours on a low heat returning every hour to skim off any more fat that may have risen to the surface. It is important not to boil, the stock. If it was to boil the fat would boil back into the stock leaving you an end result of an oily texture. After 6 hours pass the stock through a fine sieve into a container and leave to cool. Once cool, place a lid on the container and the stock will keep for 3 days in a fridge and up to 2 months in a freezer.

RED WINE GRAVY

Makes about 600ml

1½ litres meat stock

½ bottle red wine

1 shallot, peeled and chopped

100ml tomato juice

½ bulb garlic, crushed

25ml red wine vinegar

Place a heavy based saucepan on a high heat and add the garlic, shallot, red wine vinegar and red wine. Reduce by half then add the tomato juice and meat stock. Leave on a high heat and reduce the liquid by almost three quarters, or until you have a sauce consistency that coats the back of a spoon. Strain through a fine sieve, season, and your red wine gravy is ready to serve. This will keep in a fridge for up to 5 days.

THE FINISHING TOUCH

MINT AND PEPPER TEA

This is a great way to finish a meal in any season and can be served hot or cold.

Makes 1½ litres which will serve about 8 people

1½ litres cold water

1 bunch fresh mint

6 peppercorns

Place the water into a heavy based saucepan and bring up to a simmer. Once simmering, turn the heat down to a minimum and add the peppercorns and the bunch of mint using all the stalks and leaves. Leave the heat on minimum for half an hour then switch it off. Leave the mint and pepper to infuse in the water for 6 hours. After 6 hours strain the tea through a fine sieve into a container and keep in the fridge for up to 1 week. In winter this is perfect warmed up and served in a mug or in the summer, why not serve it in a tall glass over ice with a few sprigs of fresh mint? The perfect way to finish any meal.

Good produce is vital to me; I've been using the team at New Wave Seafood for longer than I care to remember

ACKNOWLEDGEMENTS

There are so many people to thank who have helped me, not only with this book but in my career and in life, that I could go on all day. So I'll try and keep it brief.

Firstly and most importantly, I would like to thank my parents for helping and supporting me so much; you've always believed in me and have supported every move I have made. I am forever grateful for everything you've done.

To Luisa Welch, for guiding and pushing me in the right direction throughout my career and always being on the end of a phone when I've needed advice.

To CCS and a personal thank you to Howard Bedford for supplying me with the beautiful plates and crockery in this book.

To my suppliers New Wave Seafood (and a special shout out to Andy Brown and Tim) who have supplied me with fantastic British seafood for as long as I can remember.

To Nisbet's, with special thanks to Rich, for all their great equipment and support over the years.

To Reeves Butchers – thanks for the fantastic British meat you have supplied me.

To Keith, Michelle, Tom, Al and all the Fifield Inn team for putting up with me.

To Carl, Paul, Phil and the team at Meze Publishing – thank you for helping me achieve my dream – without you guys this wouldn't have happened.

To my good friends Keith & Fliss, Andrew Burton, Matt, Martin, Darren and Josh for always being there for me … thank you.

… and last of all thanks to everyone, all of my incredible family, colleagues and anyone who has bought this book. I hope you enjoy making these recipes as much as I have enjoyed creating them.

Enjoy your dinner party.

Justin Brown